# DEDICATION

For Gary, my best art patron, cheerleader and schlepper of art stuff.

And to my girls, Kendall and Mackenzie, for bringing all kinds of color into my life.

# Layered Colored Pencil Jewelry

## A Step-by-Step Exploration of Colored Pencil on Copper

By

Mary Karg

# Contents:

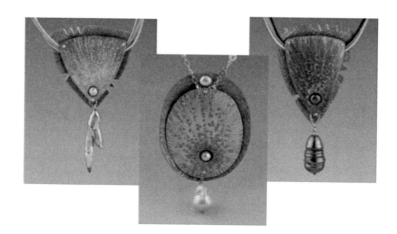

# Introduction:

Many years ago, while I was toiling away as a bookkeeper for a small computer graphics company, one of the designers told me about a place called the Contemporary Art Center. For $35, you could take a six-week course in metalsmithing. I signed up for the next session. I was so excited! I sucked. But I loved it and I was hooked. I continued to sign up for every session and I did get better. I loved the metal, but I also loved color. At the time, the only way to get color in my metal pieces was to add stones (which I love and have more rocks than I will ever use) or enamel. I tried enamel. It was not my thing. Must be a sign to buy more rocks, right?

After seven years, my husband's job took us back to Cincinnati. By then I had accumulated enough tools and supplies to set up a small studio in the basement of our new home. But during the process of searching out our new neighborhood and finding my local bead store, I discovered that the owner was hosting a weekend workshop with a glass bead maker. So, one week after the movers dropped our stuff off at the new house, I was enrolled in her class. It was a long time before my metal tools got unpacked... Fire, liquid glass and *color* became my new obsession! For a long time I was a glass bead maker only.

But somewhere along the way, metal called me again...

I live in Cincinnati. Thompson Enamels is 20 minutes across the river in Northern Kentucky. I tried enamels again. Still no...

*A*s my work evolved, it had multiple personalities: There were handmade glass beads along with beaded crochet and strung pieces. There were sterling and copper pieces with stones and glass cabs or beads to bring color in.

Then, about six years ago, I started experimenting with etching copper and brass. About this same time, I also started to notice the work of Gail Crossman Moore, Helen Shirk, Deb Karash and Marilyn de Silva. I loved the look of these artists' colored pencil jewelry and began experimenting with color myself.

In working with colored pencils, I've tried a lot of different ways to get the deepest and brightest colors possible and make the pieces durable. This book is the product of what I have learned so far. The method I offer here is certainly not the only way to apply colored pencil to metal, but this method works every time and is fast (no waiting for gesso to dry overnight). It is not suitable for high-relief stampings or etched copper and that will become apparent as we get started.

Enjoy!

Mary

# 2  Tools & Materials:

I am a self-confessed tool junkie. My dad, the electrical engineer, always maintained that if one of something was good, three was best. I have wholeheartedly embraced my dad's philosophy. I have a particular fondness for hammers and power tools (trying to save my hands). With that being said, I have tried to pare down the list of tools to a manageable level for this book. The great thing about these projects is that you don't have to have a lot of tools. While some are essential, the others can go on your wish list.

## Shaping & Texturing Metal:

There are all kinds of ways to get your sheet metal cut into the shape you want. My current favorites are the **Joyce Chen Kitchen Shears**. They will cut through metal up to 22 gauge thick and are super sharp. There are other good shears out there (I like my giant Klenk aviation shears for cutting pieces of metal off a larger roll or sheet), but these work great.

I am fairly proficient at sawing with a **jeweler's saw**, but I seldom do it. My work tends to be more simple in form and none of the projects in this book requires a jeweler's saw. However, it can come in handy if you want to make more complex shapes.

I love the **stencils** from **Art Clay World**. So many to choose from! I have also been known to make my own shapes by drawing on a plastic coffee can lid and cutting it out (this is what I did for the butterfly wings in project 8). The plastic of the lid is a perfect thickness and is more durable than a paper stencil.

We will also use a variety of **dapping blocks** and **punches** to give our pieces dimension. I like these wooden ones. Use a rawhide mallet with these. They are light enough to travel with and come in many sizes and shapes. I also use the metal ones in my studio. We also use a **bracelet mandrel** for one of our projects, but actually an aluminum can or any round hard object will do.

Plain sterling sheet metal is, in my humble opinion, somewhat boring. There are many ways to put some pizazz in your work. A basic chasing hammer can add interest easily. There are also many lovely texturing hammers available, too, as well as a multitude of metal stamps. Another, although expensive, way to get texture into your metal is to roll it in a rolling mill. I currently own a Pepe brand rolling mill and use it quite often. Another wish list item.

# Tools & Materials:

I have a small **belt sander** that I use quite often. My hands are already suffering from several decades of making things, so whenever I can use a power tool, I do. But all the project pieces in this book can be refined with old school files, sandpaper and steel wool.

I also have a small hydraulic press from **Potter USA** as well as many of their **pancake dies**. The press and dies make short work of consistently getting the same shape every time. You might add these to your wish list.

My **Wiss Notcher** is also a tool I use all the time. Originally designed for the HVAC industry, it takes quick and uniform little bites out of the edges of my pieces. Micro-Tools has the last supply of USA made Notchers.

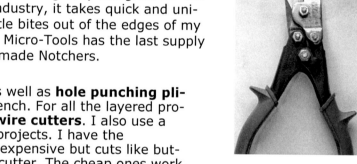

Assorted **jeweler's pliers** as well as **hole punching pliers** are invaluable on your bench. For all the layered projects you will need a pair of **wire cutters**. I also use a **disc cutter** for many of my projects. I have the **Swanstrom** brand, which is expensive but cuts like butter. **Pepe** also makes a nice cutter. The cheap ones work, but the holes require quite a bit more clean-up on your part.

## Rotary Tools:

*One of the secrets to riveting, I have found, is making sure the drill bit matches the size of your rivet. Use this chart to the right as a guide.*

I use my flexible shaft rotary motor for so many things. (I confess I actually have five of them. Did I mention I was a tool junkie?) I use it to drill, sand, polish, carve, and by changing out the hand piece with a hammer hand piece, I use it to rivet. Using the **Foredom hammer hand piece** actually revolutionized my work. It's particularly useful for riveting delicate pieces.

| Gauge | Drill Bit # |
|-------|-------------|
| 10 | 38 |
| 11 | 43 |
| 12 | 46 |
| 13 | 50 |
| 14 | 51 |
| 15 | 52 |
| 16 | 54 |
| 17 | 55 |
| 18 | 56 |
| 19 | 60 |
| 20 | 65 |
| 21 | 66 |
| 22 | 70 |

There are many brands of flex shafts out there. **Harbor Freight's Chicago Brand** is inexpensive, but the motor is too small for the hammer handpiece. I have two **Euro-tool** models and one **Foredom**. Foredom is expensive, but you won't regret spending the money on it. There are many different drill bits you can use in the versatile flex shaft. For the projects in this book we will use white silicone (coarse) polishing wheels, **Dremel's #9933** structured tooth tungsten bit, muslin and 3m satin finishing buffs and #65 drill bits. Dremel also makes a flex shaft attachment for their rotary motor. It will work also for most of the tasks in this book.

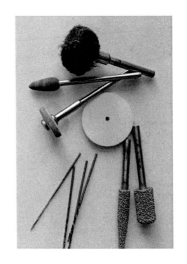

# Tools & Materials:

## Riveting:

If a **flex shaft and a hammer hand piece** attachment are not in your studio currently, all the projects can be accomplished with a **hammer** and a **metal block**. I love hammers. I was fortunate to have purchased a cabinet full of metalsmithing hammers from a local art school that was closing. Some of the hammers I have I am not sure what they are used for, but they are cool anyway. I have a small little watch maker's hammer that I like to use for riveting rather than the traditional riveting hammer. Experiment with what you have, even the basic chasing hammer will do the job.

You will also need a **metal block** for riveting and texturing. The metal block I use is so heavy it could anchor a boat, but I also have several smaller ones that travel well. I recommend getting one as large as you think your biggest piece might be.

You will need something to drill your holes into. I use a rubber block, but sometimes I need something larger and a scrap piece of 2-by-4 works great.

## Vises:

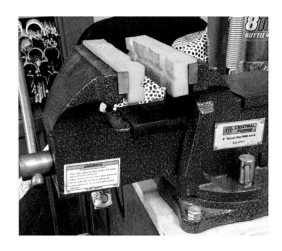

You will also need a **vise** for several projects. In particular, I use it for the fold formed project, but it comes in handy for holding bracelet mandrels and dapping punches for riveting some domed pieces. I use this small bench-top vise often and also this larger one that is mounted to my work table.

## Annealing:

None of the projects in this book require soldering. The Fold-Formed Shield Pendant, the Looped Flower Pendant and the Multi-Layered Flower Necklace will require some fire. If you add texture to your metal by hammering or rolling in a mill, it may require some softening up with a torch. One of the small **butane torches and a fire brick** will do the job nicely. If you think you might continue with more complex metalsmith projects, consider getting a Smith Little Torch or some other kind of jeweler's torch.

# Tools & Materials:

## Finishing:

I once heard an instructor say that jewelers tend to fall into two teams: team oxidize or team shiny. I definitely belong to team oxidize. If you like your pieces to be shiny and have a bright mirror finish, you may want to get a tumbler or bench-top polishing motor with wheels and compounds. For me, I seldom use anything more than 0000 steel wool or the mini-fiber wheels in fine and medium.

## Miscellaneous:

Assorted grit sandpaper, 0000 steel wool, painter's tape, assorted beads, pearls (half-drilled and full), chain, leather cording, jump rings and clasps will also be used in these projects.

## Metal:

I typically use a thinner gauge sheet of **copper** (I usually purchase my copper in the roofing department of my local home improvement store, which sells a 6-inch-by-10-foot roll for $35). It is approximately 26 gauge and is easy to cut with my shears or hydraulic press. If you want a more substantial, heavier piece, you can purchase blanks from many sources (Rio Grande, Thompson Enamels, Metalliferous, etc.) or get out your jeweler's saw and make your own custom shaped piece. I do my coloring on copper. The other layers of my pieces are either **patterned brass or sterling silver**. That is my preference for my work, but you may choose to work with other materials. I purchase patterned brass from **FDJ Tools** or **Metalliferous**. It comes in a 24 gauge size. The sterling silver is available from many jewelry supply companies. I roll it in the rolling mill or hammer it to create pattern.

## Patina/Color:

I use **Modern Masters** green patina. I've also used **Sophisticated Finishes and Jax Green for Copper** brands. All will work. I like the **Jax Black** for blackening copper. **Liver of Sulfur** will blacken copper and sterling silver. And, surprisingly, **Sharpie** permanent marker looks terrific for the blackened recesses of your pieces.

The possibilities for adding color to patterned brass are vast. **Golden Artists' Acrylics** in Fine Gold, Silver and Pearl are often my first choice. They give the brass a mixed metal appearance and tone the "brassiness" down. I also use permanent artists markers, Sharpies, acrylic paints, nail polish, alcohol inks and even spray paint.

# Tools & Materials:

## Pencils:

I only use **Prismacolor Premier Colored Pencils, Soft Core**. They were created to be very blendable and contain more wax than other brands. I haven't tried them all, but Prismacolor works the best hands down of any I've tried. I always tell people to buy as many as they can afford. You may want to use Prismacolor's colorless blender pencil, as well. (Or you can blend the colors by rubbing with your finger.)

## Rivets:

For all the projects in this book, we will use #20 solid brass escutcheon pins that I purchase from Woodworking Parts Company. I use mostly ½-inch pins, but also have a stash of shorter and longer pins. Rivets can be made from any size wire and can be made out of sterling or copper (make sure your pins are solid brass, not brass-coated stainless steel pins, which are too hard to rivet in our delicate pieces). Again, the secret is a tight fit, so check the chart in the tool section to match rivets with your wire.

## **Crimp Tubes**:

I use these tubes between the layers of metal to give the pieces of metal dimension. Readily available from many sources, I get crimp tubes from Rio Grande. You can cut your own tubing, but life is short!

## Glue:

A little drop of Super Glue Gel helps hold the pieces together when you are riveting. Get the gel and the chances of gluing your fingers together or to your flex shaft, hammer, pliers, metal block, etc., etc., are slimmer!

## Wire:

Several different types of wires are required for various projects in this book. For the pin stem (in the Feather Brooch project), I use 20 gauge nichrome wire. For the looped pendant you need 14 gauge square wire, and for the bracelet bangle I use 11 gauge round sterling wire. Additional 20 gauge wire or head pins may be necessary for hanging any pearls or beads from your pieces. In the Multi-Layered Flower project, I opted to use 18 gauge fine silver wire because of the way it balls up—which means less cleanup. I also like to use some 18 gauge square wire for making my own clasps as described in the Bonus Tips & Tricks at the end of this book.

## Mica Sheets:

For the Shadow Box project, I use a piece of this pretty natural material in the window opening

# Tools & Materials:

## Sealers:

In my work with colored pencils on copper, I have used a variety of sealers. Xim acrylic sealer has a nice semi-gloss finish, but this brand has become increasingly hard to find. Prismacolor's Final Fixative, in matte and gloss work well, but Prismacolor may no longer manufacture these sealers. I like Aleene's acrylic sealers the best of the ones I have recently tested. The matte sealer gives the colored pencil a really nice tooth so you can continue adding more color. Once you have achieved the amount of color you want, final seal with another coat of matte and then apply some Renaissance Wax. Renaissance Wax should be applied with a soft cloth, allowed to dry and then buffed with a clean soft cloth. Never apply Renaissance Wax directly on the colored pencil, it makes a complete mess of the colored pencil. Alternatively, for a shinier look, spray with Aleene's gloss acrylic sealer. Pym II (Preserve Your Memories) is nice but glossier than I like. Grumbacher also makes a nice sealer. If you have other acrylic sealers, give them a try. I usually add some kind of patina or paint to the back layers of the patterned brass or silver, and generally don't feel the need to seal them. If you like your metal shiny, use ProtectaClear or PYM II (Preserve Your Memories). Both work well.

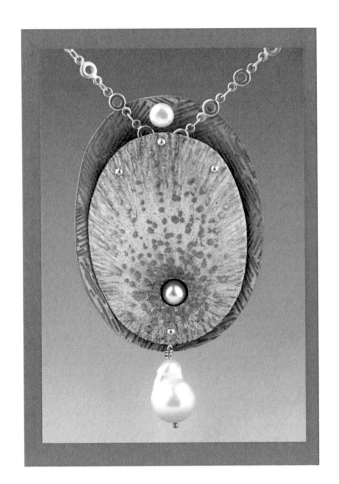

# Colored Pencil Projects

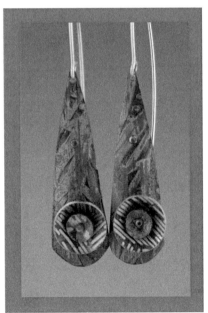

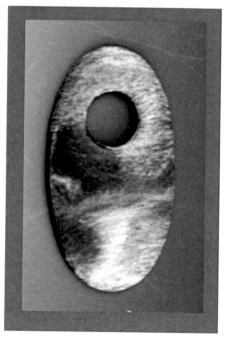

# 3  *Colored Pencil on Copper Basics*

**Basic Materials**:
- 26 gauge copper
- Green patina
- Small Paint brush
- Prismacolor Premier Colored Pencils
- Acrylic sealers, matte and gloss

**Basic Tools:**
- Metal shears
- Flex shaft or Dremel
- Polishing wheels
- #9933 Dremel structured tooth bit
- Sandpaper, files or belt sander
- Dapping block with daps
- Rawhide hammer

**Optional:**
- Hole punching pliers or
- Centering punch and #65 drill bit
- Chasing hammer

## Introduction

*W*elcome to the fun world of colored pencil on copper! This chapter covers everything you need to get started drawing on copper.

There are several different ways to apply colored pencil to metal, but I prefer this method. It works every time (color always stays on) and it's fast, since it doesn't require gesso that has to dry overnight. This method is not suitable for high-relief stampings or etched copper--I will explain why as we get into the following steps of this project.

***The first five steps in this chapter are the foundation for coloring on metal that you will use in every project***. The complexity of the projects increases over the course of the book, and techniques outlined in one project ***may*** be used in the following projects. If you prefer to not make the projects in order, you should at least read the instructions for previous projects carefully before jumping in.

# Colored Pencil on Copper Basics

## Let's Get Started

**Step 1**  Cut your desired shape from the sheet copper. For this oval, I used a hydraulic press and an oval die. However, it is easy to cut the copper with shears and then remove any burrs with a belt sander, flex shaft or files and sandpaper. I do not like rough edges in jewelry, so I run my finger around the edge of the piece to make sure nothing snags.

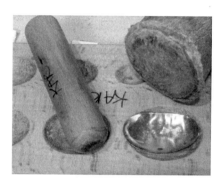

**Step 2**  After the piece is smoothed out, give the piece some dimension. (This step is optional, but I think it adds interest.) Place the piece face down in a dapping block die that is slightly larger than the metal piece. Select a punch that matches the die and gently dap the copper with the dapping punches and rawhide hammer to form a slightly curved piece. If you would like even more dimension, move your piece to the next smaller die and dap again.

**Step 3**  If you will use this piece as part of one of the following projects, now is the time to drill your holes. With a Sharpie marker, mark the hole placement on the back of the piece. I like using a centering punch and hammer to gently make a little divot in the metal. This divot gives the drill bit a place to sit so it doesn't scrape around the surface of the metal. Drill with a #65 drill bit.

*Drilling should be done **after** doming because dapping a piece can distort the holes and ruin the eventual fit of the rivet.*

# Roughing up the Metal

**Step 4** Insert a #9933 structured tooth tungsten bit into the flex shaft or Dremel, and rough up the surface of the piece. Make sure you rough up the entire surface. Giving the metal a "tooth" for the colored pencil's wax to adhere to is critical for successful coverage. It is also important to apply some pressure while completing this step. The piece should feel like coarse, rather than fine, sandpaper and should grab the skin a bit when running your finger across it. The highly abrasive bit you used in this step would have obliterated the design of a stamped or etched metal.

# Patina

**Step 5** In order for the colored pencil to stick, the metal must have patina. For this example, I used green patina rather than Jax Black. (I usually prefer the green patina for coloring and generally only use the black when I am going to color a piece black). Paint your piece with the patina using an old paint brush. I have one that is dedicated to the patina only. The patina will change the color of the copper. If you notice any bright sparkly spots, there are probably traces of skin oil. Go over the spots with the tungsten drill bit and reapply patina. If you have a stubborn spot, try getting a little aggressive with your brush and really rub the piece with it. Allow the patina to dry. You will notice the copper start to turn from "old penny" brown to lovely shades of turquoise. The patina also forms a slight crust on the metal piece.

***Note:*** *I am not sure why you need to both rough up and patina the copper, but you do. Colored pencil won't stick directly on roughed-up copper or on patina-smooth copper. No short cuts on this part, folks. Sorry!*

# Colored Pencil on Copper Basics

## Coloring

**Step 6** The fun part at last: coloring! I always start with the lightest shade or white and cover the whole piece (unless the final desired color is black, as with the Disc Earrings, Night Sky Pendant or Butterfly Wing Earrings projects shown later in this book).

Using my fingers, I rub the colored pencil into the piece. I know other artists will put their pieces in a toaster oven or use a heat gun, but our hands are hot enough. Really. It is messy, but effective. To make graduated shades of blue on this piece, I start by adding darker shades, rubbing in between each layer. **Don't rub so hard that you rub off the patina, just a nice gentle once-over to blend.**

In this example, I used the black pencil at the top to make really dark blue.

*Note: If you notice there is a spot that will not take the colored pencil, one of two things has possibly happened: You didn't get the piece roughed up enough, or the patina did not adhere. Take your tungsten bit and run over the spot thoroughly, then re-apply the patina. Allow to dry and begin coloring and blending again.*

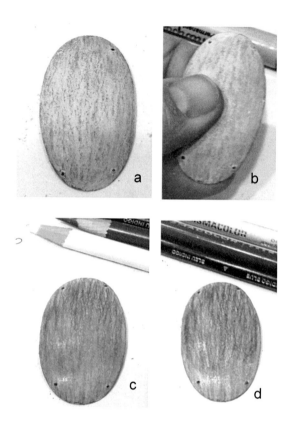

**Step 7** Prismacolor pencils are made with a lot of wax so they are more blendable than other brands. At this point, to blend all the colors, you can apply colorless blending pencil to the whole piece or use your lightest color pencil (this is what I typically do).

# Sealing

**Step 8** At some point, you may notice that the piece will not take any more colored pencil. If you want to add more color and depth to your piece, spray it lightly with matte acrylic spray. Allow the piece to dry to the touch and then gently add more colored pencil, rubbing and blending as you go.

**Step 9** Once you are done coloring, you can seal your piece. Any acrylic spray sealer will work. Depending on how you want your piece to look, use either a matte, semi-gloss or gloss, following the directions on the can. If you like a shinier piece, you can add a second coat after the piece has dried. I typically prefer a semi-gloss appearance to my work. I achieve this by spraying a coat of matte acrylic, allowing to dry and then applying Renaissance Wax. The wax should be applied with a soft cloth or fingers, allowed to dry and then buffed with the cloth. Don't apply Ren Wax directly to the colored pencil, as it contains acetone and will make a mess of your piece. Once the sealer is dry, you can embellish the piece with metallic paints or Sharpie. We will talk more about embellishing in later chapters.

**Step 10** If you want to make the back of your piece pretty, you have several options:
  1. Rough up the back, apply patina, then color with pencil as you did on the front.
  2. Rough up the back a bit with steel wool and leave the pretty shiny copper color.
  3. Rough up with steel wool and apply alcohol inks or nail polish to add a bit of color, or Jax Black for Copper for a completely black back. Jax Black should be sealed with Renaissance Wax.

# 4 *Birch* Trees Colored Pencil Oval

**Basic Materials**:
- 26 gauge copper
- Green patina
- Small Paint brush
- Prismacolor Premier Colored Pencils
- Acrylic sealers, matte and gloss

**Basic Tools**:
- Metal shears
- Flex shaft or Dremel
- Polishing wheels
- #9933 Dremel structured tooth bit
- Sandpaper, files or belt sander
- Dapping block with daps

**Optional:**
- Hole punching pliers or
- Centering punch and #65 drill bit
- Chasing hammer

## Introduction

*I* love drawing these little birch trees, even though I'm usually terribly embarrassed by my drawing skills (which are limited and often don't see the light of day). I use this little landscape scene in a lot of my pieces and it was one that inspired Kaska Firor to take the oval piece and make a wire woven frame to wear it as a pendant.

## Let's Get Started

**Step 1– 5** Start this project in the same manner as described for the basic oval in chapter 3.

**Step 6** For the trees, draw lines with a white pencil to form trunks. Try to make them random along the horizon. Those in front will be bigger; the ones in back will be skinnier and smaller. Varying the size of the trunks gives the illusion of depth in the forest. Add branches on the trees.

**Step 7** Add beige to the trees, overlap and blend with the white of the trunks, but don't totally cover. Rub the trees with your fingers to really set the wax in the copper.

**Step 8** Start coloring the sky with the lightest blue. Color between the tree trunks and approximately 3/4 of the way down the trunk where the grass line would appear. Then add the darker colors, remembering to overlap and blend but not totally cover the lighter color. Finish up with a few lines of midnight blue. Blend with a white or sky blue pencil. Overall, a sky blue, a medium blue and a midnight blue are sufficient for this gradation. Blend the layers with your fingers.

**Step 9** As you did with the sky, color the grass from light to dark, blending and overlapping a bit of the sky and tree trunks to look like blades of grass. Next, start adding more blades of grass with your different colors of green to get a pleasing natural look. Keeping your pencils sharp makes this detail work easier. Blend as you go.

**Step 10** Go back over your trees with white and beige pencils to define.

# *Birch* Trees Colored Pencil Oval

**Step 11** With a sharp black pencil, make small horizontal marks, some straight lines, some small 'v's randomly on your trees. Make some more lines with a dark brown pencil. Overlap some of the dark brown lines with black marks; make others separate.

**Step 12** If you are happy with your coloring, seal with matte or gloss acrylic sealer. I often like to add more color, so at this point I spray my piece with matte sealer. When the piece is dry I add more color to different areas of the piece to add depth. Finally, I seal with matte or gloss acrylic sealer.

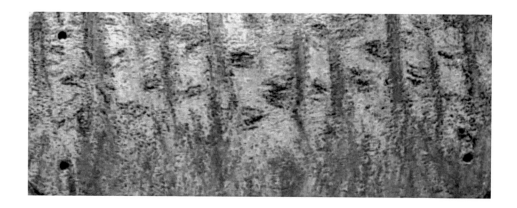

*Woven Wire Pendant by Kaska Firor with Birch Tree Colored Pencil Drawing on Copper by Mary Karg*

# 5 *Birch* Trees Layered Pendant

**Materials**:
- 26 gauge copper
- 24 gauge patterned brass
- Small pearl. either fully drilled or half drilled
- Chain or leather cording
- Clasp
- #20 brass escutcheon pins,
- 2mm gold colored crimp tubes
- Green patina and Liver of Sulphur
- Sharpie markers
- Small Paint brush
- Prismacolor Premier Colored Pencils
- Acrylic sealers, matte and gloss

**Tools:**
- Metal shears
- Flex shaft or Dremel
- Polishing wheels
- #9933 Dremel structured tooth bit
- Sandpaper, files or belt sander
- Dapping block with daps
- Metal bench block
- Flush cutting wire pliers
- Rawhide hammer
- Centering punch and #65 drill bit
- Chasing/riveting hammer or hammer hand piece for flex shaft

**Optional:**
- Golden Acrylic paint in Iridescent Pearl
- Nail polish
- Metal sealer (such as ProtectaClear)

## Introduction

*L*ayering the colored pieces elevates the drawing and turns it into an elegant work of wearable art.

***Note: You'll use the following steps for layering for all of the remaining projects in this book.***

## Let's Get Started

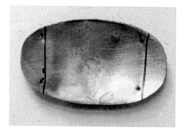

**Step 1-5** Cut an oval piece of copper as in chapter 3. Follow steps 1-5 in that chapter to prepare your piece for coloring and drilling. For this piece, I drilled four holes in the oval copper piece to make the piece sturdy. The top rivets will act as anchors for the chain.

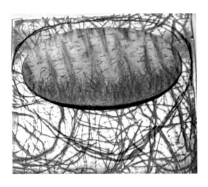

**Step 6** Select a piece of patterned brass or silver for the back. In this example, I used patterned brass that I ran through a rolling mill. If you don't have access to a rolling mill, you can achieve some really nice textures with hammers and stamps.

Using your oval as a guide, draw on the brass around the top of the oval approximately 1/8-inch larger (or whatever looks pleasing to you) and draw a freehand point on the bottom. The shape looks a bit like a spade or a heart on the bottom. Make the point at the bottom large enough to rivet a pearl there.

**Step 7** Using your scissors or shears, cut out the back piece.

**Step 8** Refine the edges smooth using a belt sander, flex shaft or files and sandpaper.

**Step 9** If you choose, add some kind of patina to your patterned metal. In my example, I lightly painted the surface with Golden Acrylic paint in Iridescent Pearl. While the piece was still wet, I wiped off the excess, leaving some paint in the recesses of the pattern. If you choose to use sterling, you can use Liver of Sulfur or Sharpie marker and sand with 600 grit sandpaper to bring up the pattern. Other paint, nail polish or markers can be used to add some color to your brass back plate. Allow to dry and then sand with 600 grit sandpaper. If you like to keep your brass shiny, seal with a metal sealer such as ProtectaClear or Pym II.

# *Birch* Trees Layered Pendant

**Step 10** As we did with the copper piece, dome the back piece in the dapping block, working from the back.

## Assembling the Piece

**Step 11** Using the top copper piece as a guide, tape it down over the silver/brass back plate on a scrap piece of wood or rubber block. Begin drilling the holes in the back piece. Put the brass escutcheon pins in the holes to hold in place as you go. This will ensure that the piece will not slip out of alignment. Once the holes are drilled, remove the tape, then mark, punch and drill the hole for the pearl. Remove the pins so you can color the top copper piece.

**Step 12** If you haven't already colored a birch tree oval, follow steps 6-12 in chapter 4, color and seal your copper piece.

**Step 13** Thread the pins back through the holes in the copper piece, put a small drop of super glue gel at the base of the pin on the back side. Slide the crimp tube down over the pin on the back side. Make sure the pins are as straight as possible when allowing the glue to set up.

**Step 14** Once the glue has set up, thread the pins through the back plate. To set the fully drilled pearl I chose for this example, it had to be riveted, not glued. (The pearl's hole was too small for the pin and had to be enlarged. I did this using a #65 drill bit while keeping everything wet. See **Bonus Tips & Tricks on page 108** for more information on drilling pearls.) If you're using a half-drilled pearl, it will be set in the next step. Now decide how you will wear your pendant. I threaded some chain on the pins that will be riveted in the next step. You could also thread some leather cording, smaller chain or even stringing material under the pins after riveting.

## Riveting

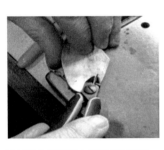

**Step 15** Working from the back of the piece on a bench block, trim the pins down with your flush wire cutters to about .5mm. Making sure you have good contact with the metal bench block, begin ***gently*** hammering the pin to flare the metal out beyond the perimeter of the hole. If your fit is snug, you don't have to work hard to get the metal to flare over the hole. Instead of a traditional riveting hammer, I use a small chasing hammer or a watch maker's hammer.

If you haven't done any riveting before, practice on some scrap metal to get the hang of it. I invested in a hammer hand piece for my Foredom Flex Shaft that acts like a tiny jack-hammer and does all the work of riveting. It is particularly useful when riveting delicate things like glass beads. (If you like the process of cold connections, save your pennies— the Foredom hammer hand piece is totally worth the price). Rivet your pearl or, if you are using a half-drilled pearl in your piece, thread the pin through the hole from the back of the brass or sterling silver layer, trim the pin, place a small amount of glue on the pin and insert the pin in the pearl's hole. Allow to dry.

**Step 16** Clean up the back of the piece with a silicone wheel or sandpaper to smooth the rivets. Steel wool or polish the back. Add color if you like with ink or nail polish. Add a clasp to your chain. I often make my own clasps to blend in with the chain. See the **Bonus Tips & Tricks (page 108)** for instructions on making a simple clasp.

# *6 Layered Colored Pencil Pendant with Pearl*

**Materials**:
- Basic materials from page 23
- 26 gauge patterned sterling silver or 24 gauge patterned brass
- Small, slightly flattened pearl either fully drilled or half drilled
- Chain or leather cording
- Clasp
- #20 brass escutcheon pins
- 2mm colored crimp tubes to match back plate

**Optional:**
- Golden Acrylic paint in Iridescent Pearl
- Sharpie Markers or Alcohol Inks
- Metal sealer (such as ProtectClear or Pym II)
- Liver of Sulfur

**Tools:**
- Basic tools from page 23
- Disc cutter
- Centering punch
- Chasing/riveting hammer or hammer hand piece for flex shaft
- #65 drill bit
- Sharpie marker (extra fine tip)
- Metal bench block
- Flush wire cutting pliers
- Steel wool

**Optional:**
- Rolling mill or hammers or stamps
- Notcher

## Introduction

$I$n this project, you will create a double-layered triangular shape with a small opening for a pearl to peek out, but as you can see in the Gallery of Work on page 115, all kinds of shapes and multiple layers can be employed to produce unique and beautiful pieces using the following steps. I am particularly fond of adding a little peek-a-boo hole for a small pearl to nestle down into. Feel free to omit this element if you desire, but keep in mind that flaring an opening is a useful and versatile technique to practice and have in your bag of tricks.

**Step 1** Using a template of your choosing (or a shape drawn on paper) and a Sharpie, trace the shape on the copper. If you need a small hole for a half drilled pearl, mark its placement before cutting out the shape.

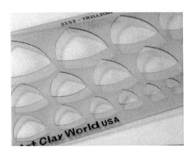
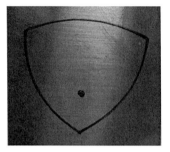

**Step 2** Using a disc cutter, cut out a hole that is slightly larger than the pearl.

**Tip:** I have found cutting this opening out first can save a lot of aggravation. If the hole ends up not perfectly centered with the piece, you can redraw the shape according to the placement of the hole and then cut it out.

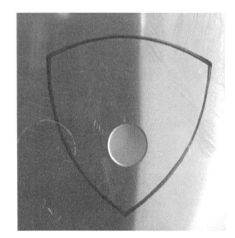

**Step 3** Using shears, cut out the shape and refine the edges with sandpaper, files or a silicone wheel on the flex shaft.

# *Layered Colored Pencil Pendant with Pearl*

## Shaping

**Step 4** Center and then tape the hole over a die in the dapping block that is slightly larger than the opening of the hole. With a corresponding punch, hammer the opening to slightly curve and flare the edges of the hole. This gives the piece a more interesting and dimensional appearance.

**Step 5** Using a larger dapping block and working from the back, dome the whole piece. Use smaller punches around the hole opening so as to not flatten your nice curves.

# Roughing up the Metal

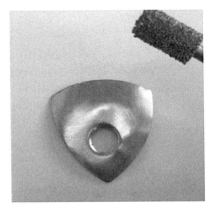

**Step 6** Using a tungsten bit rough up the surface of the copper piece (refer to Colored Pencil Oval Basics Chapter 2).

**Step 7** As we did in Chapter 5, mark on the back of the piece where you are going to place your rivets—in this example, I put one in each corner of the triangle. Center punch the divots, then drill the holes with a #65 drill bit.

# The Back Plate

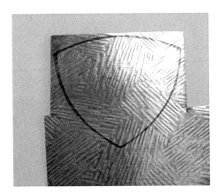

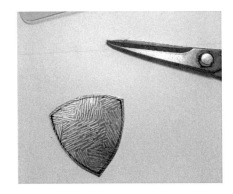

**Step 8** Using the same template as in step 1, trace a shape for the brass or silver back plate that's about 1/8-inch larger than your copper piece and cut it out. In this example, I used patterned silver that I ran through my rolling mill for the back plate. If you don't have access to a rolling mill, you can achieve some really nice textures with hammers and stamps. I then Liver of Sulfur the piece and lightly rub with 600 grit sandpaper or steel wool to bring out the design. Sand the edges smooth and dome the piece in the dapping block.

# Layered Colored Pencil Pendant with Pearl

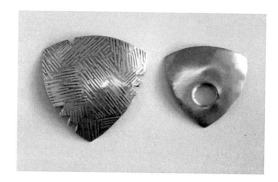

**Step 9** I often use a notcher to make small little bites out of the edges of the back plate. On this particular piece, I put three notches on one side, two on the second side and one on the third side. File and sand smooth. Don't have a notcher? You can achieve the same effect with scissors, you just have to use a little more care to make the notches uniform.

## Drilling & Riveting

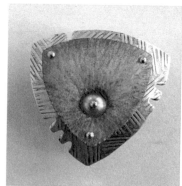

**Step 10** Tape the copper piece in place on the silver or brass back plate. Place the taped pieces on a rubber block or scrap piece of wood. Insert the drill bit in the hole of the copper piece and begin drilling the holes in the brass back plate. Put the brass escutcheon pins in the holes to hold the front and back pieces in place as you go. This will ensure that the pieces of metal will not slip out of alignment. Once the corner holes are drilled, remove the tape and mark and drill the hole for the pearl. You are now ready to color your copper. Follow the directions in steps 1-5 of chapter 3. For this piece, I colored light to dark green radiating out from the opening of the hole. Start by coloring the entire piece with the lightest color and gently rub and blend as we did in chapter 1. Proceed by adding the darker shades, leaving some of the lighter colors uncovered to achieve the ombre, graduating color, effect.

**Step 11** When your copper piece is colored, sealed and dry, follow the directions in chapter 5 for assembling the pieces together and riveting. In my example, I am going to hang the pendant from some metallic leather cording, threading them under the pins before riveting.

## Painting

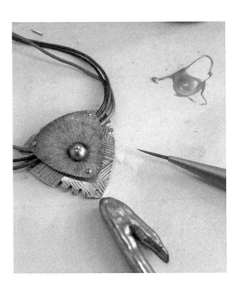

**Step 12** Finally, after all the riveting is finished, I like to add some bling to the colored pencil. Here I used a small amount of Golden Acrylic paint in Iridescent Silver Fine (Iridescent Gold Fine and Iridescent Pearl Fine are also really nice) and made small dots radiating out from the pearl. Did I mention I like weird pearls? I punched a small hole in the bottom of the silver back plate with hole punching pliers (a drill can also be used) and dangled a pearl with a head pin. This dangling bit is optional of course, and left to your own devices and imagination, you can make your pendant look any way you want.

# 7  Triangle Disc Earrings

**Materials**:
- Basic materials from page 23
- 26 gauge patterned sterling silver or 24 gauge patterned brass
- Earring findings
- Super Glue gel
- #20 brass escutcheon pins
- Sharpie marker (extra fine tip)
- Liver of Sulfur or Sharpie marker to darken silver
- Jax Black for copper

**Tools**:
- Basic materials from page 23
- Disc cutter
- Centering punch
- Chasing/riveting hammer or hammer hand piece for flex shaft
- Metal bench block
- Flush wire cutting pliers
- Steel wool, sand paper, Flex shaft or belt sander

**Optional:**
- Rolling mill, texturing hammers or stamps

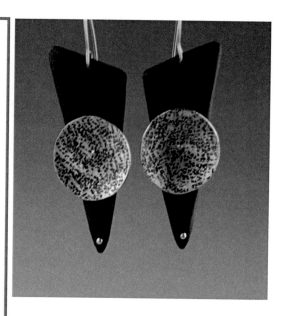

## Introduction

*T*hese are fun and fast earrings and can be adapted to any shape or color you want. In this chapter, I address how to rivet a curved surface and give you an alternative to Liver of Sulfur to get the deepest black on copper.

## Let's Get Started

**Step 1**  Begin by cutting two back plates out of the copper. I love this unconventional triangle shape with its rounded corners, but really, any shape will do.  Cut out two discs. In this example I used 1-inch sterling silver discs cut with a disc cutter, but you can use a stencil to trace circles and cut them out with scissors. Refine all four shaped pieces and smooth their edges.

**Step 2** I opted to use a texturing hammer on the sterling silver discs but, again, it is up to you. If you hammer and the discs become very hard, you may want to use a torch to anneal. You may also need to refine the disc edges again if they get out of shape from hammering.

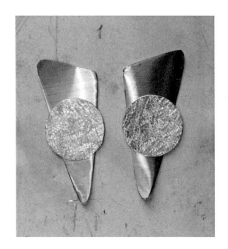

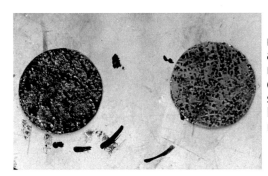

**Step 3** I like to patina the disc in some manner to make the pattern pop. In this example, I used a black Sharpie permanent marker to color the entire surface of the discs. Once the marker dried, I used 600 grit sandpaper to remove the marker from the high points of the discs, allowing the black to remain in the recesses.

**Step 4** On the patterned side of the discs, mark the center with a marker and center punch a divot as in step 6 of chapter 6.

# Triangle Disc Earrings

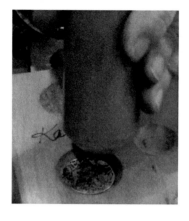

**Step 5** Place your discs in a corresponding die on your dapping block pattern side up. Dap. Then move the disc down to the next smaller depression and dap again to get a deeper curve.

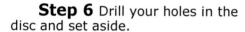

**Step 6** Drill your holes in the disc and set aside.

Shaping

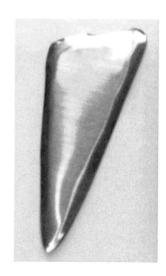

**Step 7** I decided to round the edges only of my triangles instead of overall doming. To round the edges, place the edge of the triangle on a metal block allowing it to hang over slightly, approximately 1/8 inch. Using your rawhide mallet, begin gently hammering to bend the copper over the edge of the block. Align the corners of the triangle with the corners of the block and gently hammer them also. You can also use you flat nose pliers to curve the metal edges so that they are nice and even. Repeat the rounding process on edges of the other triangle. When you shape the second triangle, make sure the triangles are mirror images of each other and not facing the same direction (because that just looks weird!).

## Roughing up the Metal

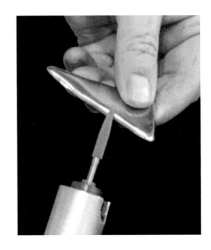

**Step 8** Begin roughing up the copper triangles with a tungsten bit, taking care to get the edges completely roughed up. Rough up the back with some #0000 steel wool.

## Patina

**Step 9** Pour a small amount of Jax Black for Copper in a plastic cup and drop your triangles in. If you don't have Jax Black, you can use Liver of Sulfur or the green patina. I love Jax though, and really recommend it for blackening copper. Allow the pieces to completely turn black on the front and back. If you have a spot that will not turn, rinse and dry the piece, then hit it with the bit again (or steel wool if the spot is on the back) and put it back in the solution. Once the pieces are completely black, rinse them with water and dry.

## Drilling

**Step 10** Mark the holes for drilling on the back of the triangles. I put the triangles side by side and eyeballed the hole placement, but if you are not confident about doing that, use a ruler to measure. I drilled a hole on the top for the earring finding, one in the middle for the disc, and one on the bottom of the point for a decorative rivet.

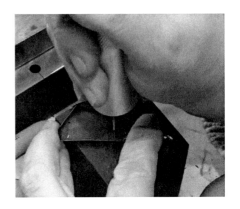

# *T*riangle Disc Earrings

## Coloring

**Step 11** Begin coloring the triangle with a black colored pencil. Rub the pencil into the piece as in steps 1-5 of chapter 3. Keep adding more pencil and rubbing until the piece looks and feels completely smooth and black.

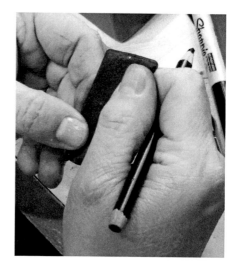

**Step 12** Seal the triangles with acrylic matte or gloss acrylic sealer and allow to dry.

## Riveting

**Step 13** Insert a pin in the bottom hole, trim and rivet.

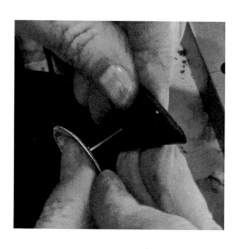

**Step 14** Insert a pin in the sterling discs. Place a small amount of super glue on the back of the disc and pin and insert in the hole drilled in the center of the triangle. Allow the glue to set up and dry.

**Step 15** Select a metal dapping punch that roughly fits the curve of the disc and set it vertically in a vise.

**Step 16** Place the piece face down on the punch as shown in this photo. Making sure the head of the pin at the center of the disc is making good contact with the punch, trim the pin and rivet. Repeat on the second earring.

**Step 17** Hang pieces from your favorite earring findings.

# 8 Butterfly Wing Earrings

**Materials**:
- Basic materials from page 23
- 24 gauge patterned brass
- Two small flat pearls fully drilled
- Earring findings
- Super Glue gel
- #20 brass escutcheon pins
- 2mm gold colored crimp tubes
- Sharpie marker
- Golden Acrylic paint in Iridescent Pearl Fine and small paint brush
- Liver of Sulfur

**Optional:**
- Metal sealer (such as ProtectaClear or Pym II)

**Tools:**
- Basic materials from page 23
- Disc cutter
- Centering punch
- Chasing/riveting hammer or hammer hand piece for flex shaft
- Metal bench block
- Flush wire cutting pliers
- Steel wool, sandpaper, flex shaft, belt sander

## Introduction

*I*'ve mentioned my dad, the engineer and tool junkie, but my mom also influences my work. She, among many things, is a master gardener and volunteers at her local park in the butterfly house. She loves all things with wings, but her fondness for the monarch butterfly has worn off on me

In the first part of this chapter, I demonstrate how I draw a monarch wing. They are an artistic version and not intended to be an exact rendition of the species. There are so many types of butterflies and moths—if you're looking for reference images, get a book or start a Pinterest board (mine is called "Things with Wings"). You can also just decorate these wings in whatever way you like.

The second part of this chapter shows how to make layered earrings, but you can use the basic steps to make a lovely pendant, pin or bracelet, too.

## Let's Get Started

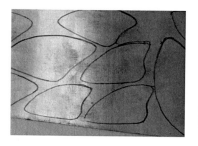

**Step 1** Using the template on page 112 (or your own shape), trace two wings on your copper. Cut out the wings and refine the shape.

# The Back Plate

**Step 2** Cut two wings, approximately 1/8-inch larger than the copper wings, out of patterned brass or sterling (again see templates on page 112). Don't forget to make them mirror images of each other. Refine the edges.

**Step 3** Apply patina, if desired, to the back plates of patterned metal. In my example, I used brass and added Golden Acrylic paint in Iridescent Pearl. When dry, I lightly sanded the pieces with 600 grit sandpaper to bring up the high points of the brass.

# Doming

**Step 4** Dome all four pieces using oval dapping blocks as in step 2 of chapter 3.

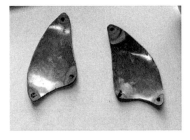 

**Step 5** Mark the location for the rivet holes on the back of both copper pieces with a Sharpie, center punch a divot for each hole, then drill with a #65 drill bit.

# Butterfly Wing Earrings

## Drilling

**Step 6** Tape the copper wings down on the patterned back plate. For the earrings, I place them dead center, however, when I make a pendant, I place the copper top piece low enough so that I can rivet a pearl on top and use that rivet to hang my chain.

**Step 7** Using the copper piece as a guide, drill the rivet holes in the back plate, anchoring with escutcheon pins as you go. Center punch and drill a hole (or use your hole punch pliers) for the earring findings.

## Roughing up the Metal

**Step 8** Separate the pieces and rough up the copper with a #9933 structured tooth bit.

**Step 9** Apply the green patina as in previous chapters and allow to dry.

# Coloring

**Step 10** Start this project with a black pencil to draw the outlines of the butterfly wings. Color all around the edges and then draw a curved line to define what would appear to be the top and bottom wings on a resting butterfly.

**Step 11** Next add the veins. Gently rub the pencil into the copper piece. Try to avoid smearing the black into the uncolored sections as much as possible. Some smearing is unavoidable, so don't panic.

**Step 12** With a white pencil, begin coloring the sections in, followed by yellow, orange and red. I like the sections to have an ombre appearance; the darker colors fade into the light from top to bottom. Carefully rub the pencil with each layer, again taking care to avoid smearing as much as possible. I like to go back and add some more white and yellow. This enhances the ombre appearance and blends the colors nicely.

# *B*utterfly Wing Earrings

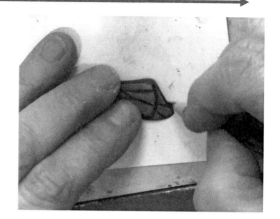

**Step 13** When you are happy with the coloring of the sections, go over your black lines again with a sharp black colored pencil.

**Step 14** If you are satisfied with coloring, seal the pieces with gloss acrylic spray. If you would like to add more color, spray with matte, allow to dry, then add further coloring. Add a final coat of acrylic spray sealer.

## Assembling & Riveting

**Step 15** Rivet the pieces together as in step 13 of chapter 5: Insert the pins, glue the crimps, assemble the pieces together, trim and rivet.

# Painting

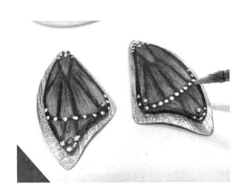

**Step 16** Monarchs have little white dots along the rims of their wings. I paint on dots with Golden Acrylic paint in Pearl.

**Step 17** I like to use marquise shaped ear wires, however they are a thicker gauge than most of my pearls, so I drilled the pearl holes to enlarge them. (See Bonus Tips & Tricks on page 112 for tips on this process.) Insert the pearl and form the loop at the bottom of the finding. Drill or punch a hole for the finding on the back plate, then attach the wings to the findings.

**Optional**: If you want to make a pendant, insert a pin in the pearl and put the pin through a link in your chain behind the pearl. Then put the pin with the pearl and chain through the hole in the back plate and rivet. Add a clasp.

# 9 Evening Sky Tri-Level Pendant

**Materials**:
- Basic materials from page 23
- 26 gauge patterned sterling silver
- 24 gauge patterned brass
- Small, flat pearl
- Super Glue gel
- #20 brass escutcheon pins
- 2mm gold and silver colored crimp tubes
- Black Sharpie marker
- Chain and clasp
- Golden Acrylics paint in Iridescent Gold Fine
- Liver of Sulfur

**Tools**:
- Basic tools from page 23
- Centering punch
- Chasing/riveting hammer or hammer hand piece for flex shaft
- Metal bench block
- Flush wire cutting pliers
- Scrap wood or rubber block
- Vise
- Assorted small paint brushes

## Introduction

$U$sually my work tends to be oversized and somewhat funky; this next project is as close to elegant as I get. Originally designed as a long pendant, you could certainly funk it up if you wanted to make it bigger. I particular like the versatility of the multiple metals. I'd like to try the Keum Boo method of fusing thin layers of gold to silver, but this project gives a similar appearance and is so much easier and less expensive. This project is also an exercise in adding a third layer and building in a bail without solder.

**Step 1** Following the templates on page 112, start by cutting out a long triangle of copper that tapers to a blunt end (technically a trapezoid).

**Step 2** Cut the slightly larger triangle out of patterned silver for the back plate.

**Step 3** Cut the small spoon or lollipop shape out of patterned brass. This piece will eventually be used to create the bail.

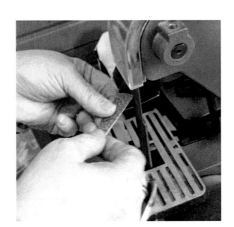

**Step 4** Refine your shapes and shape the spoon piece if it's uneven. I use a belt sander for refining, but a flex shaft with a sanding disc or a coarse white silicone wheel will do the job also. Or you can always go old school with files and sandpaper.

## Doming

**Step 5** Give the triangles some dimension by placing them in a grooved doming block. If the triangles are longer than the block, take care to gently hammer so as to not cause a crease where the pieces hang over the block.

# Evening Sky Tri-level Pendant

**Step 6** Dome the circle of the "spoon" shape by placing the round part in a matching, slightly larger round die in the block. Dome with a corresponding punch. A crease in this is ok, as it will be the back of the piece and it actually helps define the piece. It really looks like a spoon now. If doming the spoon has bent the "handle", use pliers to straighten it.

**Step 7** Follow the instructions for preparing the copper for applying colored pencil (chapter 3, steps 1-5). I used Jax Black for copper instead of the green patina. Don't worry if you don't have it, the green will work fine, but you may have to apply more layers of color than I did.

# Drilling

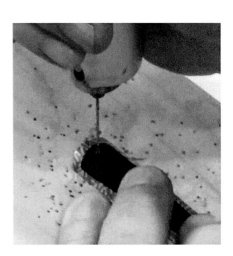

**Step 8** Mark, punch and drill two holes for the rivets on the copper front piece, one at the top and another at the bottom of the piece. Using this as a guide, tape the copper piece to the patterned sterling silver plate and drill the holes using the pins to anchor in place.

**Step 9** The back "spoon" piece needs two rivets to keep it from spinning around. I typically use the top rivet of the triangles as one and hide the other under the under the copper piece. Mark the second hole placement on the sterling piece, punch and drill. Tape the brass spoon piece to the sterling silver plate and drill those holes, using a pin to anchor.

**Step 10** Mark, punch and drill the hole for the pearl.

# *Evening Sky Tri-level Pendant*

## Coloring

**Step 11** Begin coloring your copper piece with the black pencil. Rub in the color and layer until you get the deepest and smoothest black. Seal with acrylic spray and allow to dry.

## Assembly

**Step 12** Rivet the brass spoon piece to the silver back piece first so the rivets are hidden behind the top copper piece. Insert a pin in the hole in the silver back piece. Place a small drop of super glue gel on the pin and thread the brass spoon piece on. (Don't add a crimp, because we want these layers to be flush). Only rivet the bottom hole.

Following steps 13-15 in chapter 5, insert the pins in the copper piece, glue, add crimps and thread through bottom piece(s). Allow the glue to set up, then rivet.

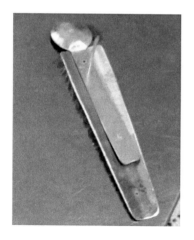

# Forming the Bail

**Step 13** Once the rivets are completed, polish up the back and using some round nose pliers, gently roll the back piece of the handle up on itself to form a bail. Glue or rivet the pearl at the top of the piece.

# Painting

**Step 14** To embellish your piece with paint, using a small brush and a dollop of Golden Acrylic paint in Iridescent Gold Fine, make small overlapping, alternating strokes on the bottom of the triangle, about a third of the way up. Then make random small dots for stars at the top of the piece, fanning out in a pleasing way. Allow to dry and thread your favorite chain through the bail.

**Note:** Now that you know how to layer three metal pieces and form a bail, you can alter the shape and size of this piece in whatever way you like. Keep in mind that larger pieces may need more rivets to keep them securely layered. For instance, a wider triangle might call for two rivets at the top—one in each corner of the triangle—and a third rivet at the bottom.

# 10 *P*en & Ink Flower Necklace with Looped Dangle

## Materials:
- Basic materials from page 23
- 26 gauge patterned sterling silver
- Super Glue gel
- #20 brass escutcheon pins
- 2mm silver colored crimp tubes to match back plate
- 7 inches of 14 gauge sterling silver square wire
- 4mm sterling jump rings
- Chain and clasp
- Small, flat stone bead or pearl
- Black Sharpie extra fine marker
- Chain and clasp
- Golden Acrylics paint, Iridescent Gold Fine
- Liver of Sulfur

## Tools:
- Basic tools from page 23
- Centering punch
- Sharp edge texturizing hammer
- Chasing/riveting hammer or hammer hand piece for flex shaft
- Metal bench block
- Flush wire cutting pliers
- Scrap wood or rubber block
- Vise
- Butane or other jewelry torch
- Fire brick
- Round nose pliers

## Introduction

*I* have to confess that this necklace happened by complete serendipity and has become one of my favorites. I painted the patina on a copper oval to make one of my traditional birch tree pendants and then got distracted by something. When I came back, the patina had turned the copper the most amazing array of colors. I almost left it alone and just sealed it to see what would happen. Worried that it would not stay those beautiful colors, I decided to use the design as a guide for my colored pencils.

The colored oval turned out pretty but kind of non-descript. I had been noticing pen and ink drawings on Pinterest and decided to draw a sketchy little flower on top of the colored pencil. Viola! Just what it needed in my opinion.

Any kind of drawing on your oval would look nice, but I recreate my pen and ink drawing in these instructions so you can have that trick in your bag.

# Let's Get Started

**Step 1** Begin by following steps 1-5 in chapter 3.

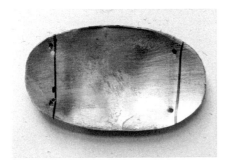

**Step 2** Center punch four rivet holes at the side top and bottom of the oval and drill. Set aside.

**Step 3** Using patterned sterling silver, cut out an irregularly shaped back plate that's approximately ¼-inch larger than the oval, allowing space for a riveted garnet or other stone bead or pearl along one side of the back plate.

**Step 4** To round the edges of the back plate—instead of doming—follow the instructions in step 7, Chapter 7 of the Triangle Disc Earrings. Place the edge of the back plate on a metal block allowing it to hang over slightly. Using a rawhide mallet, begin gently hammering to bend the silver over the edge of the block. You can also use flat nose pliers to shape the edges so that they are nice and even. Refer to Chapter 7, Step 7 for a refresher on this step if needed.

# *P*en & Ink Flower Necklace with Looped Dangle

## Drilling

**Step 5** Tape the copper piece to the back plate and drill holes for rivets, inserting escutcheon pins as you drill.

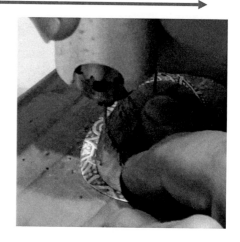

**Step 6** Center punch and drill holes on your back plate for the hanging chain, loop and stone.

## Coloring

**Step 7** Begin coloring the copper piece. If the patina you applied in step 1 did not give you a fantastic array of colors, don't despair: Pick out a light pink, blue, purple, orange and green (or any of your favorite color combinations). Color irregular patches randomly on the piece, then blend.

**Step 8** Pick out darker, more intense shades of your colors and add them to the patches, taking care to not completely cover the original lighter colors. Blend again and begin adding the next darker shades until you are satisfied with your piece. You can go back and add some of the lighter shades on top to give the piece more depth and interest.

**Step 9** Seal with a matte acrylic sealer. Add more colored pencil if desired and seal with the final gloss.

**Step 10** When the sealer is completely dry (give it at least 15 minutes), draw your flower on the top of the copper piece with an extra fine Sharpie. **Do not seal again,** as this will cause the Sharpie ink to run and ruin your colored piece.

## Assembling & Riveting

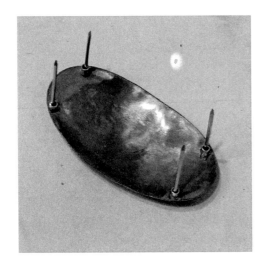

**Step 11** Thread the escutcheon pins through the holes in the copper piece, put a drop of glue at the base of the pin on the back of the copper piece and add a crimp tube. Allow the glue to dry and insert the pins through the back plate and rivet. Rivet your pearl or stone bead in the corner.

# *Pen* & Ink Flower Necklace with Looped Dangle

## Forming the Wire Dangle

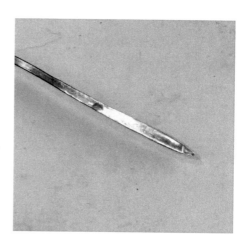

**Step 12** To create the spiral that hangs from the piece, you will need wire and a hammer of some sort. (I use 14 gauge square wire and a sharp end texturing hammer.) Begin hammering one end of a 7-inch piece of wire flat with the larger flat end of your hammer. Using sandpaper, files or a flex shaft, taper down the end a bit to create a graceful point.

**Step 13**  You may notice the hammering has made the wire very rigid and hard. Fire up your torch and anneal the metal to soften it. (I use a butane torch and a fire brick.) Heat up the wire so that the color on the wire follows the flame. There's no need to heat the wire to cherry red, because you risk melting it. Quench and dry the wire. (Always dry metal pieces thoroughly so your metal tools don't get wet and rust).

**Step 14**  To form the loop, grab the end of the point with round nose pliers and make a spiral.

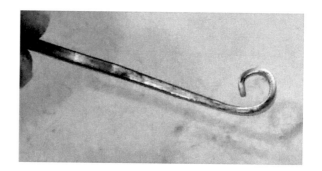

**Step 15** To texture the sides of the wire, strike along the edge and then flip and texture the opposite side. I only do two sides, just because I like the way it looks. Feel free to texture all of the sides if you like. You can also leave the wire plain, use metal stamps or use a chasing hammer for texture.

**Step 16** Making sure the textured edges are facing what will be the front and back of the piece, begin forming a couple of curves in the wire. If curving the wire is difficult, anneal it again.

**Step 17** Wrap a complete loop in the wire next. Then a couple more curves. Bend the wire so that it forms a wide "V" shape.

**Step 18** Hold your wire up to your piece to be sure it's long enough to span the distance between the two bottom holes.

# Pen & Ink Flower Necklace with Looped Dangle

**Step 19** Trim your square wire so that approximately ¾ inch is left for the other loop. Hammer flat and shape this end into another graceful point. Roll this end into a spiral also.

**Step 20** If at any point the wire seems too hard to manipulate, anneal, quench and dry.

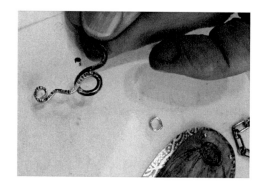 

**Step 21** Make any adjustments you'd like to the wire's shape. Liver of Sulfur, wash, rinse and dry, then use steel wool or fine grit sandpaper to bring up highlights.

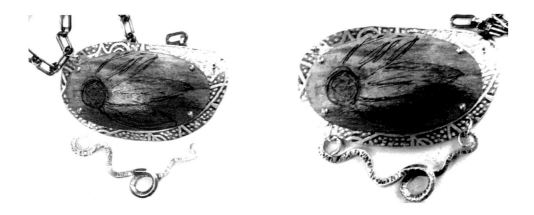

**Step 22** Attach the loop to the bottom holes with jump rings. Attach a chain to the top and add a clasp.

# *11* Foldformed Shield Necklace

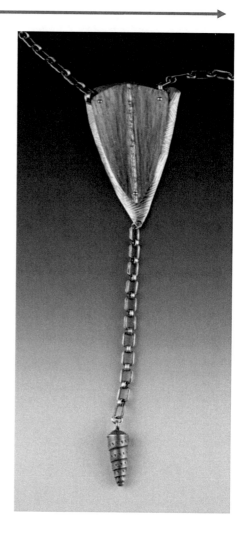

**Materials:**
- Basic materials from page 23
- 26 gauge patterned sterling silver
- Super Glue gel
- #20 brass escutcheon pins
- 2mm silver colored crimp tubes
- Black Sharpie marker
- Chain
- Sterling silver, pearl or other type of drop bead
- Golden Acrylics paint in Iridescent Silver Fine
- Liver of Sulfur

**Tools:**
- Basic tools from page 23
- Centering punch
- Sharp edge texturizing hammer
- Chasing/riveting hammer or hammer hand piece for flex shaft
- Metal bench block
- Flush wire cutting pliers
- Scrap wood or rubber block
- Vise
- Butane torch
- Fire brick
- Round nose pliers

**Optional:**
- Notcher

## Introduction

*F*oldforming is a lot of fun and such a versatile technique. For this project we are going to do a simple fold and texture. If you are interested in learning more, check out Charles Lewton Brain's book **Foldforming** or watch his online video on Craftsy. He came up with this technique and his work is amazing.

I have chosen to do this project as a long triangle, but once the folding portion is complete, you can create any shape you wish.

# Let's Get Started

**Step 1** Begin by annealing a piece of copper (refer to page 108, in Bonus Tips & Tricks for annealing instructions). Quench in water and dry.

**Step 2** The metal should bend easily. Fold the copper in half with your fingers and then hammer the crease with a rawhide mallet.

# Foldformed Shield Necklace

**Step 3** Place the folded piece of copper in a vise crease edge up, with approximately 1/8 inch sticking up above the jaws of the vise.

**Step 4** With your sharp edged hammer, make cross marks along the length of the fold.

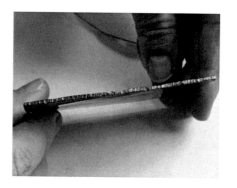

## Shaping

**Step 5** Remove the piece from the vise and cut it into the desired shape, in this case, a long triangle with a slightly curved top (I am using Art Clay World's Long Shield Template).

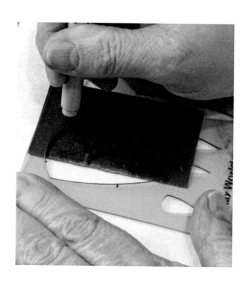

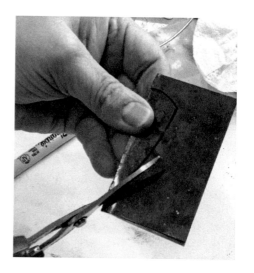

**Step 6** Your piece will have work-hardened where it was hammered. Anneal again. Quench and dry.

**Step 7** You should be able to unfold the piece easily, but if not, use a dull kitchen knife to pry the piece open.

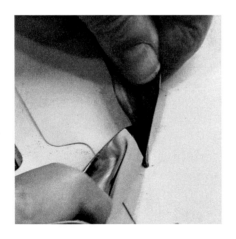

**Step 8** Refine the shape and smooth the edges.

# Foldformed Shield Necklace

**Step 9** Even though the piece has been folded, I still like to add dimension with doming. Place the piece fold side down in the dapping block and begin doming, taking care to not hit the fold. Use smaller dapping punches and go around the fold.

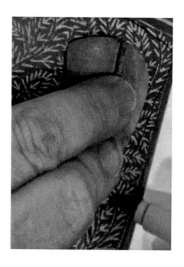

**Step 10** Cut a larger shape for a back plate, dome and patina if desired. Add any notches you may want. Rough up the folded copper piece, paint with green patina and mark and drill holes in both the copper and back plate pieces.

## Coloring

**Step 11** For this piece, I created a graduated ombre effect similar to the coloring in chapter 3, only in green shades. Color lighter shades on the top, then graduate down to darker shades at the point. Seal with acrylic spray.

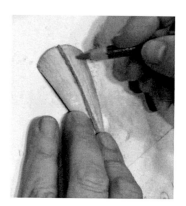

**Step 12** Rivet the two layers together with brass escutcheon pins and crimp tubes, adding chain at the top corner rivets if desired. Add a clasp or make the chain long enough to fit over the head.

## Finishing Up

**Step 13** I wanted the fold to stand out and mimic the silver in the back plate, so I used my finger to rub the fold with Golden Acrylic paint in Iridescent Silver Fine.

**Step 14** If you'd like to add a drop to your pendant, punch or drill a hole at the bottom of the back plate. Attach a length of chain with a jump ring. I used handmade sterling silver drops that had been in my stash for quite a while to make an interesting drop from my pendant. It gives the piece a kind of plumb bob look that is rather unusual, but any stone, glass art bead or pearl would look nice also.

# 12 Feather Brooch

**Materials:**
- Basic materials from page 23
- 26 gauge patterned sterling silver
- 24 gauge patterned brass
- Super Glue gel
- #20 brass escutcheon pins
- 2mm colored crimp tubes to match feather shaft
- 20 gauge nichrome wire
- Black Sharpie marker
- Chain and clasp
- Golden Acrylics paint in Iridescent Gold Fine
- Liver of Sulfur

**Optional:**
- Nail polish

**Tools:**
- Basic tools from page 23
- Belt sander or Dremel sanding drum bit or silicone wheel for flex shaft
- U-channel dapping block with daps
- Centering punch
- Sharp edge texturizing hammer
- Chasing/riveting hammer or hammer hand piece for flex shaft
- Metal bench block
- Flush wire cutting pliers
- Scrap wood or rubber block
- Assorted pliers

## Introduction

*I* love pins. I want to bring pins back in popularity. However, I hate soldering pin backs. I can't tell you how many times I have soldered pin findings shut. It is somewhat embarrassing to admit; pin backs are my white whale.

So rather than carrying on like Ahab, I decided to take the lazy girl's approach and find a way to cold connect a pin back. You'll learn my secret in this project.

I also really like birds. I find them fascinating and so beautiful. I was inspired to create this pin in the shape of a feather. After you learn how to make your own pin-back, you can turn whatever shape you want into a pin.

# Let's Get Started

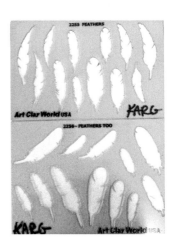

**Step 1** Begin by cutting out a feather shape. If you feel challenged by drawing your own, use the template on page 112 or the Feather template from Art Clay World. I cut out my shape first and then used a Wiss Notcher to take out little bites on a slight angle. Refine your shape and sand smooth.

**Step 2** I seem to always have little scraps of patterned sterling silver lying about. I used one for the shaft of the feather. Choose a scrap that is wide enough to accommodate drill holes for rivets. Shape your scrap to give it a pleasing curve that mimics the shape of your feather or use the template in the back if you opted to not draw your own. Refine the scrap and sand smooth.

**Step 3** For the pin back, make a small "L" shape out of brass. This piece should be roughly the same size as your feather. If you are using patterned brass as I am in this example, make the "L" shape backward so that the pattern will show. There is a template in the back for this piece also. Refine the shape and sand smooth.

# Feather Brooch

## Doming

**Step 4** To give the feather dimension, put it face down in a dapping block. Because the feather is long and thin, I use the U-channel wood block. Lay one of the wood dapping punches down along the length of the die and lightly hammer with a rawhide mallet. If the feather is longer than the channel of the block, slide it up and hammer again.

## Roughing up the Metal

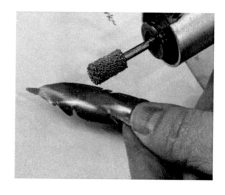

**Step 5** Rough up your copper, patina and allow to dry as in previous projects.

## Drilling

**Step 6** For this project, because the shaft of the feather is on top, we are going to mark and drill it first. Follow the template in the back, or depending on how long your pin is, drill two or three holes. These holes should not be too close to either end of the feather. Leave enough room so that the pin back is attached it will be hidden and not show from the front.

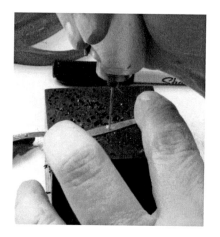

**Step 7** Using the copper feather piece as a guide, drill the brass "L," inserting pin(s) to anchor.

**Step 8** Remove the pins and tape the pin-back piece to the copper feather. Drill holes, using the pin(s) to anchor as you go.

## Coloring

**Step 9** There are so many ways to color your feather! In this example, I made the top red, transitioning to purple then to blue. As with other projects, start with the lightest colors and blend as you go. Add the darker, more intense colors and then go back to some lighter colors to blend. I drew a faux shaft of a dark burgundy on this feather to give it some shading.

# Feather Brooch

**Step 10** Seal with matte acrylic spray and allow to dry if you want to add more color. When you are happy with how the feather looks, spray with the final acrylic sealer of your choice.

## Assembling & Riveting

**Step 11** While waiting for the sealer to dry, insert pins into the sterling piece. I do not add a crimp on the very top rivet, because I think it makes the feather look more realistic to have it gradually rise in dimension. Add a drop of glue only to the bottom rivet(s) and add crimp tubes.

**Step 12** When everything is dry, assemble all three pieces together. Rivet. Take extra care to not over hammer this piece as the front sterling piece is thin and can easily bend. Sand any rough edges on the back.

## Making the Pin Stem

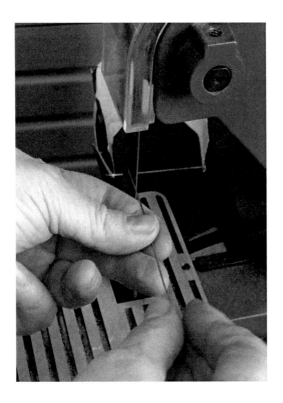

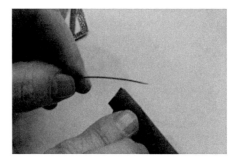

**Step 13** To make the pin stem, I use a length of nichrome wire, 20 gauge. This thin, strong wire is perfect for making a pin stem. The exact length is determined by how long your pin is: Start out with a length that is about twice as long as your pin. For this project, cut 6 inches, and we will trim the excess.

I use a belt sander to grind one end down to a sharp point. If you don't have a belt sander, you can use a flex shaft with a sanding drum bit or silicone wheel bit or files and sandpaper to create a point. Be careful to not stab yourself in the process. I refine my pin with the white silicone wheel in a flex shaft and then lightly sand with some very fine sandpaper.

# Feather Brooch

## Forming the Pin Back

**Step 14** With round nose pliers, grab the other end and roll it back on itself, forming a "U" shaped hook for the catch. Slightly curve the end upward.

## Forming the Pin Stem

**Step 15** Place the pointy end of the pin stem in the "U" shape catch, allowing about 1/2 inch to stick out beyond the brass piece. Thread the other end through the loop hinge. Wrap the wire around the loop in the brass and trim with wire cutters.

 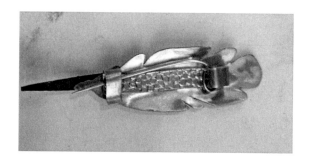

**Step 16** With needle nose pliers, make a bend in the pin stem at the base of the loop so that the pin points up and away.

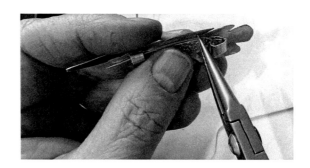

**Step 17** Using your thumb, gradually curve the pin stem back down to the catch end. This bend and curve should give the pin stem enough tension against the catch so that it doesn't slip out when worn.

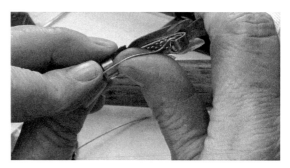

**Optional:** I decided to add some sparkly nail polish to the back for color.

# *13* Layered Bangle Bracelet

**Materials:**
- Basic materials from page 23
- 26 gauge patterned sterling silver or 24 gauge patterned brass
- Super Glue gel
- #20 brass escutcheon pins
- 2mm colored crimp tubes to match back plate
- 11 gauge sterling silver wire
- Black Sharpie marker
- Chain and clasp
- Golden Acrylics paint in Iridescent Gold Fine
- Liver of Sulfur

**Tools:**
- Basic tools from page 23
- Disc cutter
- Belt Sander or Flex shaft with sanding drum or silicone wheel bits
- Bracelet mandrel (or sturdy tin can)
- Centering punch
- Sharp edge texturizing hammer
- Chasing/riveting hammer or hammer hand piece for flex shaft
- Metal bench block
- Flush wire cutting pliers
- Scrap wood or rubber block
- 1/8-inch drill bit
- Assorted pliers
- Tape measure

**Optional:**
- Sterling silver stamp
- Muslin wheel and rouge
- Fine microfiber wheel

## Introduction

*A* bold bracelet on the wrist can make such a statement. This project can take so many directions and is surprisingly comfortable to wear: The bangle is thin and can be shaped to fit any size wrist. I am particularly fond of the butterfly and the large round disc versions. I use a sterling silver back plate in this project, but brass, gold filled or copper are also attractive. The bangle wire we'll use is round, but these bangles can be made from rectangular or half-round wire with equally lovely results.

**Step 1** Begin by cutting a shape out of copper and a brass or sterling back plate that's approximately 3/8 inch larger than the copper piece. The overall length of your back plate shouldn't be bigger than the top of your wrist. Refine and smooth the edges of both pieces.

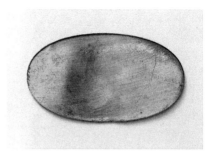

## Drilling the Holes for the Catch & Hinge

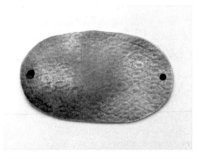

**Step 2** Before doming your pieces, decide where to place the larger holes that will be used to attach the bangle wire. Drill or punch the holes with your disc cutter. I used 11 gauge round wire for this example, so the holes needed to be large enough to accommodate the wire and have some play so that the bracelet moves easily. I used a 1/8-inch drill bit for a more than adequate opening.

# *Layered Bangle Bracelet*

## Doming Your Pieces

**Step 3** Dome your pieces. Bracelets, if worn frequently, can take a lot of abuse. I will take that into consideration with designing my piece and often make the bottom piece curve upward to offer the colored pencil layer a bit more protection.

## Preparing the Metal & Drilling

**Step 4** Rough up your copper and patina. Apply patina to the back plate, as desired.

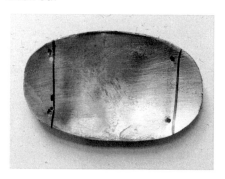

**Step 5** Mark the rivet hole placement on the back of the copper piece. It is important that the rivet holes and the top piece have enough clearance from the larger holes in the back plate so that the bracelet bangle wire will attach and move freely. Use a center punch to divot and then drill for the rivets. Tape the top piece to the bottom and drill, using the top as a guide. Insert pins to anchor.

*Tip: When the two pieces are domed in the opposite directions, it is easier to hold in place if you make a tape roll and place it under the top piece.*

# Coloring

**Step 6** Color your top copper piece as usual and seal.   Refer to the Birch Trees chapter for applying color pencil.  The birch trees make a beautiful bracelet. I have made poppy fields, butterflies wings, abstracts, landscapes and geometric doodles. Even a graduated color effect can be stunning. This time, it is a raven head...

# Assembling & Riveting

**Step 7** Rivet your pieces together as we have in previous projects, using crimp tubes to add a bit of space between layers. It may be necessary to add more than one tube on each pin so that the wire bangle has good clearance. Clean up the back of your bracelet.

# *Layered Bangle Bracelet*

## Measuring the Bangle Bracelet

**Step 8** The bangle construction requires a bit of math. Measure the size of your wrist. If you don't like tight bracelets, add a little to this measurement so that the bracelet is comfortable.

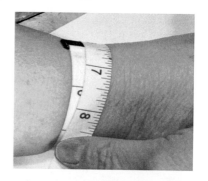

My arms have some meat on them, so my wrist measures 7 ½ inches. I add an additional 1/2 inch so the bracelet doesn't feel like a tourniquet. My assistant, Katie is 17 and an athlete, her skinny little wrists barely measured 6 inches.

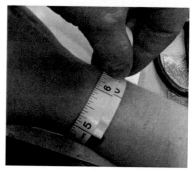

**Step 9** Measure your layered back plate from the center of each hole. Mine measured 2 inches.

**Step 10** Here's the math part: Subtract the length of the back plate from your wrist measurement. In my example, my wrist measurement is 8 inches minus 2 inches for the back plate equals 6 inches. Add back 1 inch for the loop and peg part of the bangle. So, for my example, I cut a piece of wire that measured 7 inches. (8-2+1=7). minus 2 inches for the back plate equals 6 inches. Katie's bracelet would measure 5 inches (6-2+1=5).

**Step 11** With a Sharpie, make a mark ¾ inch from one end of the wire, and another mark ¼ inch from the other end.

**Step 12** Using a belt sander, flex shaft or files, remove the metal along the length of your ¾" measurement. This should reduce your wire approximately in half. Make the reduction a smooth and gradual one. The goal is to make the round wire look like half-round wire on the end.

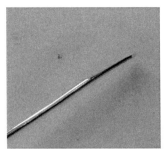

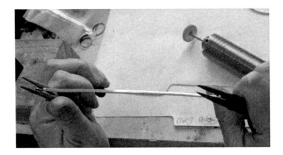

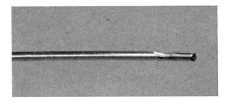

**Step 13** On the other end of your wire, begin making a notch in the wire directly on the mark. This notch needs to be directly across the wire from and aligned with your wire reduction on the other end. If it doesn't line up, you will have issues with making the bangle work properly once it has been formed. To make the notch, place the silicone wheel or your file on you mark and begin removing the metal. A small divot will begin to form. Keep removing the metal until the notch is approximately halfway through the wire. Refine and smooth the wire ends.

# Layered Bangle Bracelet

## Forming the Bangle

**Step 14** Using a bracelet mandrel, wrap the wire around and hammer with a rawhide hammer to harden and form. Make sure the reduced side is facing out.

**Step 15** If you have a sterling stamp, mark your wire on what will be the inside of the bangle (this will be the side that hasn't been filed).

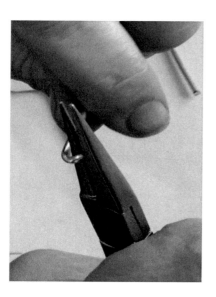

**Step 16** Using round nose pliers, bend the notched end up to form a small peg (this will act as your bracelet catch) and roll the tapered end into a loop (leave it slightly open so the layered copper and silver piece can be inserted).

**Step 17** If you like your sterling bangle to have a shiny, mirrored finish, tumble or polish the wire with a muslin wheel and rouge. I like  bracelets with a more matte surface (bracelets take a lot of abuse and end up looking matte anyway). I applied a fine microfiber wheel to the bangle to give it a soft brushed look.

**Step 18** Thread the wire loop through the hole in the back plate and close gently with pliers.  To operate the bangle, the other peg end should be easy to insert in the hole when slightly squeezed but also have enough tension so that the bracelet doesn't fall off the arm.

# 14  Shadow Box Pendant

**Materials**:
- Basic materials from page 23
- 26 gauge patterned copper or 24 gauge patterned brass
- 26 gauge copper sheet
- Super Glue gel
- #20 brass escutcheon pins
- 2mm crimp tubes
- Black Sharpie marker
- Jax Black patina
- Mica sheet
- Chain or cording with clasp
- Lichen, feathers, sticks, pearls or any other small items to enclose in the shadow box

**Tools**:
- Basic tools from page 23
- Belt sander or Flex shaft with sanding drum or silicone wheel bit
- Centering punch
- Chasing/riveting hammer or hammer hand piece for flex shaft
- Metal bench block
- Flush wire cutting pliers
- Scrap wood or rubber block
- Paint brush
- 1/8-inch drill bit
- Flat nose pliers
- Tape measure or ruler

**Optional:**
- Solder

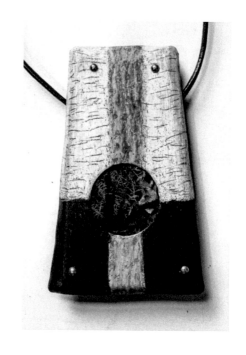

## Introduction

*T*hese little shadowboxes can be so much fun to make. This diorama with a Crackerjack toy deer surrounded by lichen and sticks creates a woodland scene. I made one with lichen, moss, small pebbles and sticks from a special place I visited as a remembrance. I've also filled one with pearls and another with crystal points. The boxes can be whimsical or serious; you could even rough up the interior of your box and draw something peeking out. I like to use mica sheets in my windows. It is thin and easy to cut into shapes. Mica also comes in a myriad of interesting patterns and colors; some comes totally transparent and others have blotches and lines of black, grey, blue, red and orange. You could easily use thin sheets of Plexiglas also, if you want a totally transparent, window-like appearance.

**Step 1** To start, determine the finished size of your box. In this example, my box will be a trapezoid when finished. To make the back and side walls of the box, I cut the shape from patterned copper (see templates, page 112). Your box could easily be a square, rectangle or a triangle.

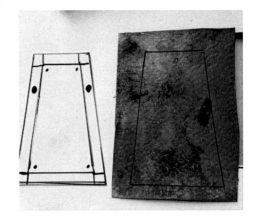

**Step 2** At each corner, measure and mark ¼-inch away from the corner. Cut the corners out of the copper square as shown in the photo.

**Step 3** Mark rivet holes in each corner, punch and drill. If you want to hang your piece from the box itself, mark and drill those holes as well on what will be the side walls of the box. It is easier to drill these holes while the piece is still flat and not in the shape of a folded box.

# Shadow Box Pendant

## Forming the Box

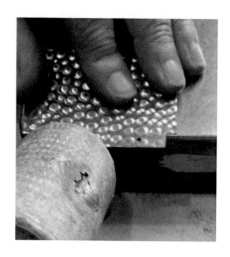

**Step 4** With a rawhide hammer and steel bench block, place your copper on the block with approximately ¼ inch of the copper hanging over the edge. Begin gently folding the copper over the corner of the block by hammering.

**Step 5** Using your flat nose pliers, begin folding the edges up along the score lines so that the corners meet and the walls of the box are formed. The box will not be completely sealed. If you want to solder the seams, do that at this point.

**Step 6** Refine the edges of the box and the corners so that there are no rough edges. I use a belt sander and a white silicone wheel in the flex shaft.

# Patina

**Step 7** You can make the box completely black by dipping it in Jax Black Patina. (Wait to seal with Renaissance Wax until after riveting, which can cause scratches that will need to be touched up.) You can also heat patina the box, use alcohol ink or nail polish for color, or leave the copper color as it is.

# Forming the Top

**Step 8** Cut a "window" in the front plate, or lid, of the shadowbox with a disc cutter. Be mindful of how large your box behind it is and make sure that the opening is smaller. For my example, I used the 10mm punch. You will also want to make sure that enough metal extends over the box to be able to have a matching drill hole for the rivet. I made my front plate 1/8 inch larger than the box and the same shape. The front plate can be any shape you may want, as long as it is sufficiently larger than the box.

**Step 9** Next we will cut out our front plate. (If you decided to not hang your pendant from the box itself, you will need to plan for some kind of bail. A loop of metal can be formed and riveted or holes can be drilled and the piece can be hung from jump rings.) Shape and refine the edges.

# Shadow Box Pendant

**Step 10** The plate needs to be relatively flat where the box attaches to it, but it can still have some dimension. Place the front piece on a bench block and gently curve the edges with a rawhide hammer. If the edges are wobbly and not smooth, carefully bend with pliers where needed.

## Roughing up the Metal

**Step 11** Rough up the front plate with a tungsten bit and paint with green patina.

## Drilling

**Step 12** Tape the box in place on the back and drill the front plate using the rivets to anchor in place as you go. I drill one corner and then drill the corner diagonally across from it. This seems to keep the piece more secure and in place.

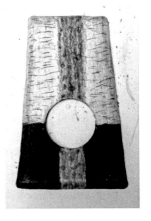

**Step 13** Color the front plate of your shadow box as desired. When you are satisfied with the coloring, spray with acrylic sealer.

## Assembling the Piece

**Step 14** Cut a piece of mica slightly larger than your box but smaller than the front plate. We want the mica to sit on top of the box and not fall down in. This is what will keep all your treasures secure in the shadowbox. Place mica down on the back of the front plate and using it as a guide, drill holes in the mica.

**Step 15** Insert the pins in the front piece, glue and thread the mica onto the pins.

# Shadow Box Pendant

**Step 16** Put another drop of glue on the pin and add a crimp tube. Depending on the depth of your shadow box, it may be necessary to add a second drop of glue and another crimp tube.

## Filling the Box & Riveting

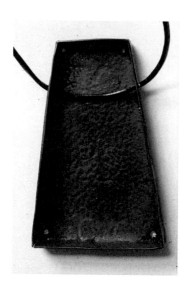

**Step 17** If you drilled holes in your box for chain or cording, insert that first and slide the box into position. Place your materials in the shadowbox. A small drop of glue may be useful in holding things in place. When the glue is dry, thread the pins through the box and rivet.

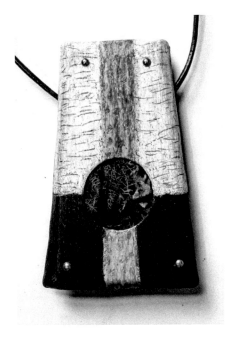

# Finishing Up

**Step 18** Clean up the rivets and apply Jax Black with a paint brush as necessary. Rub a thin layer of Renaissance Wax over your box to seal.

# *15* Multi-Layered Flower Necklace

**Materials**:
- Basic materials from page 23
- 26 gauge copper
- 26 gauge patterned and oxidized sterling silver or 24 gauge patterned brass
- #20 brass ½-inch escutcheon pins
- 2mm crimp tubes to match the metal used for the back plate
- Super Glue gel
- Black Sharpie marker
- Liver of Sulfur
- Chain or cording with clasp
- 8-inch piece of 16 gauge fine silver wire
- Golden Acrylics paint in Iridescent Silver Fine or Iridescent Gold Fine if using brass

**Tools**:
- Basic tools from page 23
- Centering punch
- Chasing/riveting hammer or hammer hand piece for flex shaft
- Bench block
- Flush wire cutting pliers
- Scrap wood or rubber block
- Wiss notcher
- Polishing wheels
- Disc cutter
- 1/8-inch drill bit
- Flat nose pliers
- Round nose pliers
- Long nose pliers or tweezers
- Heat resistant, self-locking tweezers
- Butane (or other) torch
- Binding wire
- Vise with small metal dapping punch
- Tape measure or ruler

**Optional**:
- Art Clay World Trillion Template

## Introduction

$F$or this book's final project I want to challenge you with this multi-layered piece. I have chosen this stylized flower pendant to illustrate the planning and a bit of engineering necessary to complete a more complicated piece. The center of this piece has stamens that are made with wire and a butane torch. If you would rather not play with fire, you could rivet a pearl or some other bead in the center. This piece consists of five different layers: a patterned and oxidized sterling silver back plate; a cut-out colored pencil flower shape of copper; a smaller triangular piece of patterned and oxidized sterling silver in the center; a small round disc of colored pencil on copper; and five fine silver wire stamens. This piece can also be made with patterned brass (instead of the sterling silver) with equally beautiful results.

# Multi-Layered Flower Necklace

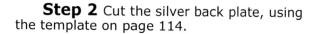

**Step 1** Start by cutting the flower shape out of copper using the template on page 114. Cut the shape of the outline first, then once it is free from the larger piece of copper, begin cutting the "petals." Refine your shape with sandpaper or a white silicone wheel on a flex shaft.

**Step 2** Cut the silver back plate, using the template on page 114.

**Step 3** If you are the type that would want each notch to be exactly equally spaced, use a ruler to mark where each notch should go. If you are more like me and usually wing it, just make a notch in each corner and then the middle of each side and then eyeball the remaining notches from there. Life in the fast lane: Woo-hoo! Clean up the notches with a silicone wheel or sandpaper, making sure there are no rough scratchy edges. If you are using sterling silver, mark the back of your piece .925.

# Adding Dimension

**Step 4** To add dimension while keeping the center of the piece relatively flat, round just the outer edges of the colored pencil flower piece and the sterling back plate (just like in the triangular earring project on page 44). Place the flower piece on a steel bench block and hammer gently with a rawhide hammer. If needed, use round nose pliers to add additional curvature. Repeat with the sterling back plate.

# The Top Layers

**Step 5** Using a disc cutter, cut out a small hole in the copper that will be in the center of the top disc. I used the smallest, 3mm punch, but a 1/8-inch drill bit works also. Punch a 10mm disc from the copper with a disc cutter so that the 3mm hole is in the center. (I have centering positioning dies for my disc cutter so that my hole is dead center of my disc.) Dome the disc, rough it up with the structured tooth bit, patina, apply colored pencil and seal as we have in previous projects. I colored mine with varying shades of magenta and purple.

# Multi-Layered Flower Necklace

**Step 6** Punch another 3mm hole out of the patterned sterling silver (or brass) sheet that you will use for the small triangle. I used Art Clay World's Trillion template to center over the hole and trace the shape with a Sharpie. If you don't own this template, draw and cut out a triangle with slightly curved sides. Cut out the triangle shape, refine the edges and dome.

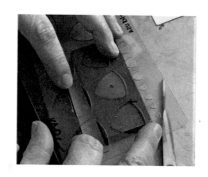

## Making the Stamens

**Step 7** Using 8 inches of 16 gauge fine silver round wire (you can also use sterling wire but I like how beautifully the fine silver wire balls up and doesn't require clean up), cut into five randomly sized pieces.

**Step 8** Bind the wire together with binding wire and hold with tungsten self-locking tweezers or other tweezers that can withstand the heat of the torch. Fire up your torch and heat the ends of the wire until a ball forms and all the pieces are melted together on one end. Quench and remove binding wire. Check to make sure that when you thread the sterling triangle onto the bundle of wires, that the ball is large enough to hold on the back and not slip through. If necessary, reheat the wire bundle and enlarge the ball.

**Step 9** Sand down the base of the ball so that it is flat and will lay nicely on your copper flower piece.

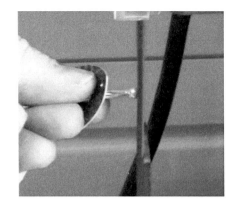

## Drilling Holes

**Step 10** On the back of the triangle, mark and center punch the placement for your rivets. These holes should be far enough away from the center hole so that the small round copper disc does not cover them, but far enough away from the corners to make it easy to rivet. Mine measures ¼ inch from the corners. Drill the rivet holes.

**Step 11** Tape the triangular sterling piece to the copper flower piece, and using the triangular piece as a guide, drill the three holes on the corners, using brass pins to anchor as you go. It's helpful to make a small mark on the back of the sterling triangle indicating which hole is the bottom one. This makes layering the pieces together go much smoother, as inevitably there is only one arrangement that works best.

# Multi-Layered Flower Necklace

**Step 12** On the back of the large copper piece, mark, punch and drill rivet holes on each "petal."

**Step 13** Rough up the large copper piece with a structured tooth bit and apply green patina.

**Step 14** Tape the copper flower piece onto the sterling back plate and drill the eight holes on the petals, using the pins to anchor, and then drill the holes where the small triangular piece will be riveted.

## Forming the Stamens

**Step 15** While waiting for the patina to dry, thread the sterling triangular piece onto the fine silver wire stamens. Then thread the small colored pencil disc on next. Grab the piece with your tweezers close to the disc. Slightly separate the wires and fire up the torch again. This time you will make a small ball on the end of each wire. Take extra care to heat each wire end separately and keep the flame away from the other wires and your colored pencil copper disc. Quench after each wire is balled up to keep the piece as cool as possible so that you don't melt the colored pencil work on the small disc.

**Step 16** If you would like the stamens to be oxidized, dip the wires only in Liver of Sulfur to blacken, taking care not to blacken your sterling triangular piece.

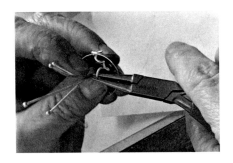

**Step 17** I randomly curled and twisted the stamens in the center with round nose pliers. You may want to tape your pliers with some masking or painter's tape to avoid marking up the wire. Curl each stamen close to the colored pencil disc piece to hold it in place. Be careful to not overwork the wire, as it can work harden and break off. If necessary, paint some Liver of Sulfur on any marks made by the pliers.

## Coloring the Big Flower

**Step 18** Color your copper flower piece as desired. In this example, I started with a light green (pale sage to be exact) and then transitioned into purples and magentas with some dark violet stripes. I have made a flower that is turquoise, orange and magenta that is very striking also. Seal and add more color until you are satisfied with your coloring. Apply a final coat of acrylic sealer.

# Multi-Layered Flower Necklace

## Assembling the Piece

**Step 19** Once all your pieces are completed, you can now add the pins and crimp tubes. Start with the three pins in the sterling triangle first and insert the pins in the holes. Take extra care that the pins are as straight as possible. Add glue at the base of the pin on the back of the triangle and add the crimp tubes. Allow the glue to set up and then thread the pins through the large copper flower piece.

**Step 20** Add a small amount of glue to each pin coming through the back of the copper piece and thread a crimp tube on the pin. Add pins and crimp tubes in this way for each petal. Allow the glue to set up.

**Step 21** Aligning all the pieces and the corresponding pins can be tricky. It's helpful to use long pointy tweezers or pliers. Just be aware that you might get a little glue on them. I hang a length of chain from each of the top two rivets for this project. Here I used 20 inches of 6mm sterling rolo chain, but any chain will work as long as it is large enough to slide over the tubes and lays relatively flat so that it doesn't add more bulk to the rivet.

Assembling all these parts can get a little unwieldy; don't try to do this when you are tired or rushing. Start with the pins at the top with the chain. Having them in place is one less thing to deal with. Then move down the piece, using your tweezers or pliers to move the pins in their proper position. Now align the three in the center and when all the pins are in place, gently pinch the pieces together. Whew!

# Riveting

**Step 21** You may find some of the rivets are more difficult to reach than others. Set up a small doming punch in your vise for those rivets that need it. I used the doming punch for the three rivets in the center and the two small petals on the edges.

**Step 23** Clean up the back of your piece and add a clasp to the chain. I used 18 gauge square wire and made a small hook clasp to mimic the look of the chain (see the Bonus Tips & Tricks chapter on page 108).

**Optional:** When the piece was completely constructed, I painted on small radiating dots of Golden Acrylics paint in Iridescent Silver Fine. Allow to dry.

# *16* Bonus Tips & Tricks

## 1. Drilling Pearls

Most small pearls have holes that are too small for #20 pins to fit through. And sometimes the hole is drilled in a different direction than how I want to use it in my piece. It's possible to drill out a larger hole by using a #65 drill bit and keeping everything wet. Dip your pearl in some cool water and swipe a small amount of water on the drill bit. Put the end of the bit in the existing hole and begin slowly drilling. When the pearl starts to feel warm or you see wisps of what looks like smoke (it's actually pearl dust and not healthy to breathe), stop and dip in water again. Repeat until the pearl is completely drilled out and the pin is easily inserted. If you are not comfortable with holding small pearls in your hand, you can hold them gently but securely with pliers or a pearl holder and drill into a piece of scrap wood or a rubber block.

# 2. Clasps

I often make my own clasps to match the design of a piece. In the Fold-Formed Shield Pendant, the sterling silver chain I used was rectangular Long and Short. To match it, I chose 18 gauge square wire to make a clasp.

Here are the steps to follow:

Hammer the very end of the wire slightly flat. Using a white silicone wheel in the flex shaft, clean up the hammer marks and smooth the end so that there are no sharp edges or corners.

With round nose pliers, curve the end up slightly. This will allow the chain to catch and slip easily into the clasp. Then I used my flat nose pliers and bent the wire in the hook shape to mimic the chain links. Cut the wire approximately 2 inches long.

Using small round nose pliers, form a small (approximately 4mm) loop. Slip the chain on to the wire and slide it down so it sits in the loop. Wrap the end around several times to close. Clean up the cut end with sandpaper or a silicone wheel. Refine the shape of the hook so that the other end of the chain or jump ring slides on easily but doesn't easily fall off.

Dip in Liver of Sulfur if you want your sterling to be oxidized and buff with steel wool.

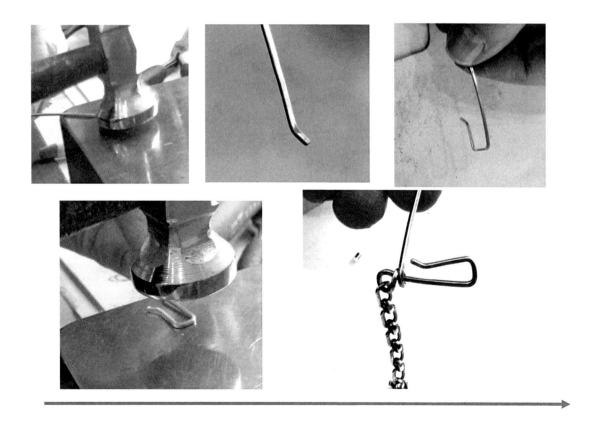

# *Bonus Tips & Tricks*

## 4 Annealing

Often in the course of working with metal, it becomes too hard and brittle to proceed. It is particularly important to start with dead soft metal when fold-forming or printing in a rolling mill. To soften, or anneal, the metal, I use a butane torch and a fire brick. I heat up the metal so that the color on the metal sheet follows the flame. I don't heat it to a cherry red, because that can cause the metal to melt. I then quench and dry the metal (make sure your metal is always dry so your metal tools don't get wet and rust). The metal will turn a dark color with oxidation. If I want to remove the oxidation, I place the metal in a pickle bath or clean up with sandpaper or steel wool.

# 5 Repairing Scratches in the Color Pencil

Scratches happen. And sometimes you just have to go back to step one and re-color the whole piece. But sometimes you can get away with repairing. If the scratch is all the way down to the copper, use a small thin brush and paint some green patina in the scratch. Allow to dry and color with your pencils, blending with your fingers as you go. If it looks like you've just scratched some of the colored pencil off, try recoloring. If you haven't used any Sharpie marker on top, you can reseal by using painter's tape to cover pearls, wire, back plate, etc. and spray the entire piece with a final acrylic sealer. It may be necessary to repaint any acrylic paint embellishments, as the spray tends to dull the paint's impact. It is also possible to spray a small amount of sealer on a postcard or other piece of scrap paper and using a small brush, quickly dip the brush into the sealer on the postcard and paint over the scratch. And sometimes, a drop or two of the acrylic paint can hide a multitude of sins….

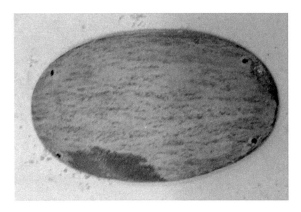

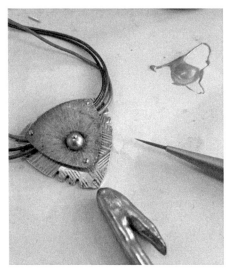

# 17 Templates

## Butterfly Wings

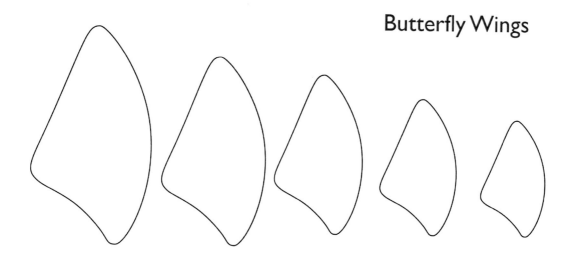

## Evening Sky Pendant

## Feather Brooch

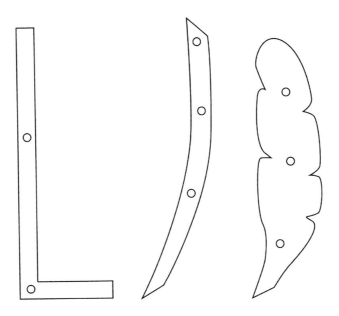

## Shadow Box Pendant

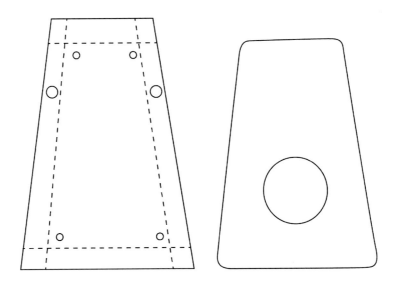

# Templates

## Multi-Layered Flower Necklace

# *18* Gallery of Work

# Gallery of Work

# Gallery of Work

# 19 Sources

**Mennards/Lowes**: #9933 Tungsten drill bits, sandpaper, copper, Dremel drill bits and accessories

**Rio Grande Jewelry Supply**: (www.riogrande.com) Liver of Sulfur, copper, dapping blocks, Foredom flexible shaft drill and hammer hand piece, 2mm crimp beads (catalog #42015713 yellow brass and #42015712 white brass), hammers, drill bits, Jax Chemicals, Swanstrom disc cutter.

**Micro-Tools**: (www.micro-tools.com) Wood dapping blocks, pliers, hammers, disc cutters, flex shaft, Wiss notchers, etc.

**FDJ Tools**: (www.fdjtool.com) Patterned brass sheet, Foredom supplies, Eurotool flex shaft, hammers, metalsmithing supplies, wood dapping blocks, etc.

**Metalliferous**: (www.metalliferous.com) Patterned Brass, wire, jewelry supplies etc.

**Potter USA**: (www.potterusa.com) Hydraulic press and dies

**Harbor Freight**: Chicago flexible shaft, sandpaper

**Woodworking Parts**: (www.woodworkingparts.com) #20 solid brass escutcheon pins, various lengths, but ½-inch most frequently used.

**Amazon**: (www.amazon.com) A wide range of items, but in particular, Joyce Chen Kitchen Shears, Wiss Aviation Notchers, Modern Masters Green Patina, Dremel #9933 Structured Tooth Drill Bit, Prismacolor Premiere Pencils

**Jax Chemical Co:** (www.jaxchemical.com) Jax Black for Copper, Jax Green Patina

**Hobby Lobby, Michaels, Dick Blicks:** Prismacolor Premiere Colored Pencils (premier soft core), green patina, acrylic spray, alcohol inks, Golden Acrylic paints, Super Glue gel

**Ebay**: (www.ebay.com) Half-drilled pearls, other odd-ball pearls

**Art Clay World:** (www.artclayworld.com) Designer templates


Visit www.MaryKargDesigns.com for project kits containing patterned brass or silver, copper, pins, crimps, 1 half-drilled pearl and 1 #65 drill bit. Sample packs of three Golden Color Metallic Paints (gold, silver and mother of pearl). Glass drop headpins also available.

# *Acknowledgements*

*I* have so many people to thank for seeing this project to its fruition. Janice Brewster, editor and maker of deadlines, thank you for keeping me on task. Kaska Firor for encouraging me to keep reaching for the next level and allowing me to ride your coattails. To The Friday Afternoon Bead Bitches, and my Cincy Incinerator friend, Lorie Burger, for their continued support and keeping it real. To Marjorie Langston and Terry Hale, for allowing me to test the waters of a broader forum of teaching in the nurturing environment of Fire on the Mountain/Hot Times. To my lovely assistant Katie Hill, for taking the great photos for this book. And Mom and Dad for always thinking my shit don't stink.

# *A*bout the Author

Mary Karg creates one of a kind art to wear from her Loveland, Ohio, studio. She designs and makes contemporary earrings, bracelets, necklaces, pendants and pins. Using a variety of materials and techniques, many pieces feature her handmade lampwork glass beads.

Mary has extensive teaching experience; working with students at The Art Academy of Cincinnati; Touch of Glass Studio, Asheville, NC; Bead & Button Show, Milwaukee, WI; Thompson Enamels, Bellevue, KY; The Bead Shop, Madeira, OH;, Beaded Bliss Designs, Harrison, OH; Bay Area Bead Extravaganza, Oakland, CA; Northern California Bead Society; Miami University's CraftSummer; Great Lakes Beadworkers Guild; as well as ongoing workshops on beadwork, flameworking and color on metal in her studio.

Mary's work has appeared in a variety of publications, including Bead & Button, Lapidary Journal, 1000 Glass Beads, 500 Beaded Objects, Beads of Glass, Glass Bead Evolution. She is a Soda Lime Times, Bead & Button Bead Dreams Competition Finalist, and was named a finalist in the ISGB Obsession Exhibit.

Mary and her husband, Gary, are currently empty-nesters and live in Loveland with their assorted furry kids.

Made in the USA
San Bernardino, CA
15 September 2017